stitches for TAILORED knits

BOOKS

XX Produced by XRX, Inc. in Sioux Falls, South Dakota, PO Box 965, 57101-0965 USA   605.338.2450   Visit us online — knittinguniverse.com   Printed in China

PUBLISHER Alexis Yiorgos Xenakis · EDITOR Elaine Rowley · MANAGING EDITOR Karen Bright · TECHNICAL EDITOR Rick Mondragon · INSTRUCTION PROOFERS Sarah Peasley, Ginger Smith · ART DIRECTOR Natalie Sorenson · PHOTOGRAPHER Lisa Mannes CHIEF EXECUTIVE OFFICER Benjamin Levisay · TECHNICAL ILLUSTRATOR Carol Skallerud · PRODUCTION DIRECTOR & COLOR SPECIALIST Dennis Pearson BOOK PRODUCTION MANAGER Greg Hoogeveen · MARKETING MANAGER Lisa Mannes · BOOKS DISTRIBUTION Mavis Smith · MIS Jason Bittner

stitches for TAILORED knits

build better fabrics
with JEAN FROST

BOOKS

Contents

stitches for TAILORED knits

Welcome

For this companion to my books, *Jean Frost Jackets* and *Custom Knit Jackets Casual to Couture*, I have selected stitch patterns that make beautiful fabrics for jackets and other tailored knits. As I researched knitting magazines, stitch collections, and pattern booklets from the 1930s to the present, I found some stitch patterns appearing over and over. Variations of these stitches produce fabrics that are wonderful in both look and feel. Others are not as well known, but offer interesting textures. I hope this modest collection is one that you will turn to again and again.

You will find these stitch patterns relatively easy to work. With a few exceptions, they only use slipped stitches, yarn-overs, increases, and decreases, and the occasional cable. When a number of these maneuvers are combined, the difficulty increases.

As you swatch your way through the collection, you should first learn the stitch, then evaluate the hand of the fabric. For achieving the fabric you desire, needle size, yarn weight and construction, and fiber content are your variables. Switch them out, one at a time, and evaluate each new swatch.

Stitch collections are often organized by techniques: knit and purl patterns, ribs, cables, lace, etc. Here, most patterns are divided into groups indicating the woven fabrics they resemble: diagonals, basketweave, or houndstooth. These are followed by a number of stitches that make wonderful fabrics using texture and color effects unique to knitting. The final section features fabrics that simulate quilting.

On page 10 in *Change It Up!*, you will see that a stitch pattern as written or charted is only the beginning. Play with it. Discover the possibilities. You can knit unique fabrics by making simple, incremental changes. When you wonder, "How about . . . ?", or "What happens when . . . ?", all you have to do is swatch. The answer is in your hands.

SWATCHING is the process that takes you from STITCH DISCOVERY through STITCH EXPLORATION then on to APPLICATION and DESIGN.

SWATCHING: THE PROCESS

Slip-stitch Basketweave

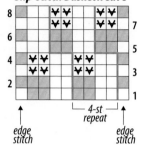

These repeat lines and brackets match for Rows 1–4 but not for Rows 5–8. Here the repeat lines are easier to follow.

MULTIPLE OF 4 + 2 EDGE STITCHES
Cast on and knit 1 row.
Rows 1, 2 K1, **[k2, p2]** to last stitch, k1.
Row 3 (RS) K1, **[k2, sl 2]** to last stitch, k1.
Row 4 K1, **[sl 2, p2]** to last stitch, k1.
Rows 5, 6 K1, **[p2, k2]** to last stitch, k1.
Row 7 K1, **[sl 2, k2]** to last stitch, k1.
Row 8 K1, **[p2, sl 2]** to last stitch, k1.
Repeat Rows 1–8.

Slip-stitch Basketweave

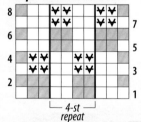

These repeat lines and brackets match and also produce the same pattern. Here, the text is easier to follow.

Cast on and knit 1 row.
Rows 1, 2 K3, **[p2, k2]** to last 3 stitches, p2, k1.
Row 3 (RS) K3, **[sl 2, k2]** to last 3 stitches, sl 2, k1.
Row 4 K1, sl 2, **[p2, sl 2]** to last 3 stitches, p2, k1.
Rows 5, 6 K1, p2, **[k2, p2]** to last 3 stitches, k3.
Row 7 K1, sl 2, **[k2, sl 2]** to last 3 stitches, k3.
Row 8 K1, p2, **[sl2, p2]** to last 3 stitches, sl 2, k1.
Repeat Rows 1–8.

Why swatch?

Determining gauge to match a pattern (or for your own design) is not the only reason to swatch. Swatching is a practical way to explore knitting — through stitch, yarn, fiber, color, gauge, and scale. It is essential for previewing the look and feel of a potential fabric. Swatching is also a way to warm up, experiment with ideas, and sketch with yarn.

The meet and greet

The process begins simply with stitch discovery. We are all familiar with this — learning the stitch and figuring out how to do any unusual techniques. We avoid frustration by practicing anything tricky *before* working it in the stitch pattern. We give you directions and, when necessary, illustrations with the stitch pattern to make this as easy as possible. You will find other, more familiar, techniques illustrated on pages 82 – 83.

Trial run

You may want to learn the stitch pattern with a basic yarn even when you are planning to knit the project in a textured yarn. The swatches on pages 22 – 81 are worked with worsted-weight wool with the same size needles — a good starting point for evaluating the stitch.

The repeat

A stitch pattern is a sequence of stitches and rows that can be repeated to build a fabric. The number of stitches to be repeated is the multiple given at the beginning of our instructions. One repeat of the rows is written and charted. Occasionally, a chart includes a second repeat of the rows to better show how two repeats fit together.

Most of these patterns have relatively small repeats, so the knitting is rhythmic and relaxing. Whenever possible, we present the charted and written repeats in a way that makes this repetition clear and understandable. Often we frame the repeat in the same way for the chart and words, but if this would make either less clear, they differ. Observe what happens as you progress from repeat to repeat and row to row in 2 examples of the same pattern (to left).

Edge stitches

I have added edge stitches (selvedges) to the patterns. When assembling a garment as I do — using a crochet hook and chain stitch to seam the pieces together — these edge stitches are essential. Without them, the first and last stitch of each row — part of the pattern — will disappear into a seam. The edge stitch can be worked either as garter stitch (always knit), or as follows: work to the last stitch, slip this stitch as if to purl with the yarn in front, then knit this stitch at the beginning of the next row. We have garter edge stitches written into the instructions and drawn on the charts. In some cases however, you will notice that the swatch was knit with slipped-stitch edges rather than with garter stitch. The choice is yours.

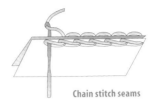

Chain stitch seams

Selvedge
the edge stitches: the first and last stitch of every row

1-stitch garter selvedge

Start small to get acquainted

Cast on and work 3 to 5 repeats of both stitches and rows to learn the stitch.

More is more!

For project-planning purposes, a swatch should be large enough to reveal the hand of the fabric. *Hand* refers to the characteristics of the fabric revealed by holding it in your hand. How does it feel? If you hold one side or corner does the fabric drape, or is it rigid? Is it limp or, if tugged gently, does it resist just a bit? Our swatches (shown at nearly full size) measure from 7 to 10 inches wide. A swatch of this size could easily become the beginning of a sleeve or one of the fronts of a vest, cardigan, or jacket.

RS

Right side *(RS) the side of the fabric visible when the garment is worn*

WS

Wrong side *(WS) the inside of the garment*

Sometimes wrong is right
Look at the wrong side. Do you like it? Is it more interesting than the right side? Again, this is *your* call.
With each stitch swatch, a turned-up corner gives a peek at the wrong side. Sometimes we feature a larger photo of a wrong side that we find particularly interesting.

Just one more swatch

You be the judge

It is *your* knitting, so this is *your* judgment call. Keep in mind that comparison is the easiest way to make a judgment. While it may be difficult to decide whether a single swatch is what you want it to be, it is much easier to recognize which of two swatches looks and feels better. Remember — swatching is a process, so don't stop evaluating until you have completed the process and are happy with the result.

It's all relative

Not happy with the fabric? What don't you like? Before you rip out, put the stitches on hold and read on. Change what you think is wrong and start another swatch. After a couple of inches, compare. You may decide to change another variable and swatch again. Repeat as needed to move in the direction you sense is best.

Other considerations

Will special edge treatments or borders be needed for structure, or are they just a design feature? Test options on your swatch, and then decide.

Not enjoying the stitch?

Would you prefer another way to work a maneuver? Say a 1/1 Right Cross with or without a cable needle? Exchange one decrease for another?
Maybe the yarn or fiber isn't a good fit for the stitch pattern?
Perhaps you want to use a different knitting needle? Different composition? Different point? Different size?
If you are comfortable holding the yarn several ways — in either hand — try another way.
Are you tired, surrounded by distractions, or being interrupted? Try again when you are well rested and have a nice chunk of quiet.
If you still don't enjoy the stitch, choose another.

Bath time

After binding off, measure the swatch, then give it a gentle wash, let it dry, and measure again. In addition to being really clean, the yarn will have relaxed into the structure of the stitch. This can make a real difference, for now the swatch is truly a fabric and you can consider its hand and drape.

Continue to evaluate the fabric, then refine, measure, wash, re-measure, and re-evaluate until you feel it is just right. Then it's time to recognize your success and relish the power!

Swatching station

We all know that empty feeling — we finish a project and there is nothing waiting in the wings. We wonder what to knit next. Newton's law reminds us that an object in motion stays in motion, but an object at rest stays at rest. Make inertia work *for* you! Before your next opus, warm up with a swatch in a new stitch or a different yarn. Soon you'll be well on your way to new inspiration. The problem will then be deciding which idea to knit first.

Organize your swatch library

Our system, developed to display the swatches at STITCHES events and in trunk shows, may also work for you. Label an index card (large or small, you decide) with stitch name, page reference, yarn, needle, and any extra details, then attach it (staple, or punch and stitch) to the swatch. A series of related swatches (sharing a common stitch, color, yarn, repeat size — whatever works for you) can be stored on a ring. Several rings can hang on an S (or other) hook to avoid the out-of-sight-out-of-mind syndrome. Of course, many systems — photos on a smart phone, pockets in binders, folders in files — can be used effectively. Just pick one, so your swatches keep working as stimuli to your continued involvement with the knitting process.

Now the fun begins

Whether you want to continue the exploration now or later, if you enjoyed knitting the swatch, then the stitch pattern is one that is worth adding to your repertoire. You can turn to it the next time you just want to play with yarn.

Continue to explore

Change yarn: substitute a color, add another, chose a different texture and fiber, adjust the value contrast. Page through *Change it up!*, pages 10–21, to see stitches being transformed just by changing what you put on the needles.

From swatch . . .

What makes a fabric suitable for a tailored knit?

• A little more substance than usual. The ball band usually offers a stitch gauge for stockinette fabric. Our mixture of knits and purls and/or slipped stitches, often within the same row, makes the stitch-to-row ratio denser. When that ratio is close to or smaller than the standard stockinette ratio of .71 (5 stitches to 7 rows), you have achieved a jacket-worthy fabric.

• Edges that don't tend to curl require minimal edge finishes, and that's a plus for clean and simple garment construction.

• Relatively small repeats make it easy to shape and size garments.

Stitch/Row to 1"	Ratio of S/R
4 / 6	.66
4.5 / 6	.75
4.5 / 7	.64
5 / 7	.71
5 / 8	.62
5 / 8.5	.59
5.5 / 7	.78
5.5 / 8	.69
5.5 / 9	.61
5.5 / 10	.55
6 / 6	1.00
6 / 6.5	.92

Practical considerations

BY THE BOOK How much yarn is required in total? The first consideration is the stitch-to-row ratio of the swatch. Our chart showing yarn requirements for a basic Chanel jacket in a range of gauges can be a help. If your stitch is garter-based or has many slipped stitches, your swatch may have more rows per inch than appear on this chart. Say you're getting 5 stitches and 9 rows to the inch and making a size 40 jacket. Our chart shows 1175 yards needed at 5 stitches and 7 rows. To estimate how much more yarn you will need at 9 rows, divide 9 by 7 (approximately 1.3) and multiply this by 1175: 1175 × 1.3 = 1528, so allow for at least 1600 yards (or whatever your comfort zone is).

FROM THE SWATCH Then there is another approach. With an accurate kitchen or postal scale, weigh the balls of yarn before and after making a good-sized swatch. The difference will tell you the amount of yarn used. Divide each difference by the total weight of the swatch to calculate the percentage for each yarn.

Or divide the weight by the number of square inches of fabric in the swatch to determine how much yarn is required for each square inch of your project. You can also extrapolate the amount of yarn by dividing the total area of the jacket by the area of the swatch, then multiplying the result by the weight of your swatch.

Yardage for Basic Jacket

SIZE	36	38	40	42	44	46	48	50	52	54
4 stitches/ 6 rows	900	925	1000	1025	1125	1150	1250	1275	1375	1425
4.5 stitches/ 7 rows	950	975	1075	1100	1200	1225	1350	1375	1475	1500
5 stitches/ 7 rows	1050	1075	1175	1200	1275	1350	1475	1500	1625	1650
5.5 stitches/ 8 rows	1150	1175	1300	1325	1450	1475	1625	1650	1775	1800

FIGURING THE PERCENTAGES But what if you are using 2 yarns? Many of the patterns use 2 rows each of 2 or 3 colors, so this is very easy math.

When colors change every row or two and there are 2 colors: 50% A, 50% B.

When colors change every row or two and there are 3 colors: 33% A, 33% B, 33% C.

When A alternates between 2 colors and B remains 1 color: 25% A1, 25% A2, 50% B.

You get the idea.

As you plan a garment, one of the first considerations is how much yarn you will need. This will vary based on the size of each stitch, the number of stitches in each square inch, and the number of square inches in your garment. This chart shows estimated yardage for the Master Jacket Pattern from Jean's book Custom Knit Jackets in each of the standard sizes and gauges. Use it as a starting point.

stitches for TAILORED knits

. . . to garment

Mirror, mirror

A diagonal can travel across a jacket…

… or mirror at the center. Simply rearrange the rows or change the decrease and the stitch sequence.

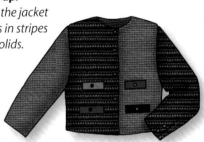

Balancing acts

MULTIPLE OF 3 + 2 + 2 EDGE STITCHES

This translates to a repeat of 3 stitches + 2 edge stitches + 2 additional stitches that keep the pattern centered and symmetrical.

Mix it up!
Work the jacket pieces in stripes and solids.

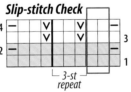

Slip-stitch Check

In the spotlight
Color reversal often can change the look of a pattern, especially when one acts as a background and the second as a highlight. Color percentages can make a difference.

Chatelaine, page 72, with colors for A and B reversed.

Change It Up!

The stitch pattern — a particular arrangement of knits, purls, slips, and other maneuvers — is just the beginning. Let's play with the yarn and see what happens.

TINY HOUNDSTOOTH, page 45

This swatch was knit with the traditional light and dark contrast. To make it more "today," **I changed the colors**, working with purple and bright pink.

Change from value contrast to color contrast

BIG HOUNDSTOOTH, page 46

Keeping the light and dark contrast, **I added a textured yarn**. I used white knitting worsted and black mohair. The mohair adds texture and lightness to the fabric, making it more interesting to the eye and the touch.

Change from color contrast to value contrast, and soften the contrast with a mohair yarn

stitches for TAILORED knits

ROYAL QUILTING, page 79

I knit the original in bright blue and pink so the structure of the pattern would be obvious. First, **I removed color contrast and added texture**. For a woven look, I chose a cotton and linen bouclé and knit the overlay with one strand each of fingering-weight wool and mohair held together. Then, I went one step further and **swatched with a high contrast** brown mohair over the same bouclé.

Keep texture contrast and add value contrast

Remove color contast and add texture contrast

HALF LINEN STITCH, page 37

The original in brown wool produces a lovely stockinette fabric with slipped stitches. **Using 2 colors of yarn** and working 2 rows of each color, produces a tweedy fabric. A heather used with a multi gives the fabric a woven tweedy look.

Make the first color a heather and the second a multi (plies of several colors)

Add a second color, working 2 rows of each

stitches for TAILORED knits

CLUSTER STITCH, page 54

This stitch resembles the Trinity Stitch, but is not as textured and is easier to knit. If you **add another color** and alternate rows, a really beautiful fabric appears. **Add still another color** for a richer, more intricate look.

Add a color, changing color on WS rows

Add 2 colors, changing color on WS rows

TRINITY STITCH, page 56

Knit in charcoal gray it makes a nubby fabric — highly desirable for a jacket. **Add a second color** for a stripe pattern, which is not my favorite. **A third color**, however, adds much more interest. This is why knitting a series of swatches is important — some work well and others not so well.

Add a color, changing color on WS rows

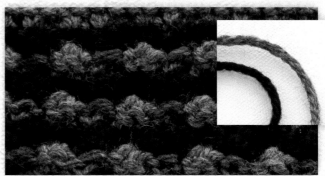

Much more interest when you add 2 colors, changing color on WS rows

SPECKLE RIB, page 58

Here we play with the stitch pattern as well. You will find charts for each variation on page 59. This fabric, combining knits, purls, and slips, is effective in solid brown. **Add a contrasting color**, teal, for the 2 slipped-stitch rows and the fabric starts to bloom. **Add a third color**, beige, and the fabric seems more intricate. I went back to 2 colors and used a multi-colored metallic yarn for the dots.

Add 2 colors, changing yarns every RS row

Add 1 color, changing yarns every RS row

stitches for TAILORED knits

Then **I tried a series of ideas** using gray mohair and white wool:
• the basic stitch pattern
• not staggering the dots
• working in garter stitch between the rows of dots.
I also swatched in a blue cotton-linen blend and variegated wool — quite pretty
in the basic pattern. Or maybe if I slipped 2 stitches instead of 1 and repeated
this twice before knitting blue rows… a lovely new look… something different!

Change to light/dark value contrast, changing pattern from staggered dots (bottom) to aligned dots (middle) to working garter stitch instead of stockinette between rows of staggered dots (top)

2 textures (a mohair blend and a metallic) in 2 colors, (a solid and a multi), changing yarns every RS row

Changing to softly variegated wool and blue cotton-linen blend and changing pattern: slipping 1 stitch for 4 rows before working all stitches in blue

15

GARTER SLIP, page 63

Garter stitch interrupted by slipped stitches makes an interesting fabric. **Add a second color** and a striking new fabric appears. **Add a third color** for a more complex fabric. Each of the 3 colors is worked for 2 rows.

Add 1 color, changing on RS rows

Add 2 colors, changing on RS rows

stitches for TAILORED knits

Next I swatched with a sport-weight yarn in brighter colors to produce lighter-weight fabrics with more punch — that all coordinate.

Change to brights and a lighter-weight yarn

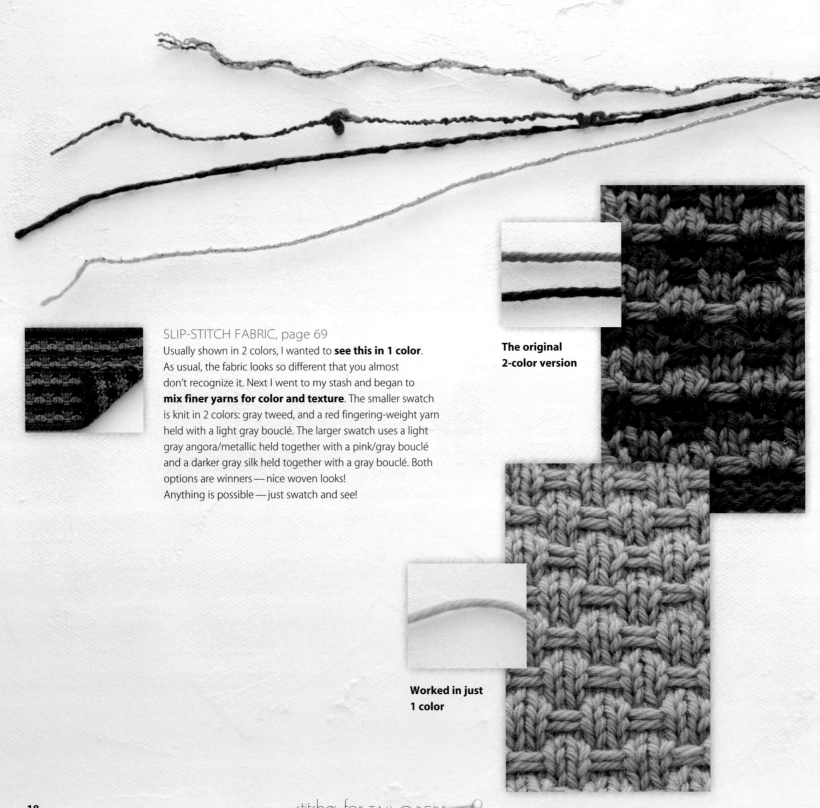

SLIP-STITCH FABRIC, page 69

Usually shown in 2 colors, I wanted to **see this in 1 color**.
As usual, the fabric looks so different that you almost
don't recognize it. Next I went to my stash and began to
mix finer yarns for color and texture. The smaller swatch
is knit in 2 colors: gray tweed, and a red fingering-weight yarn
held with a light gray bouclé. The larger swatch uses a light
gray angora/metallic held together with a pink/gray bouclé
and a darker gray silk held together with a gray bouclé. Both
options are winners — nice woven looks!
Anything is possible — just swatch and see!

**The original
2-color version**

**Worked in just
1 color**

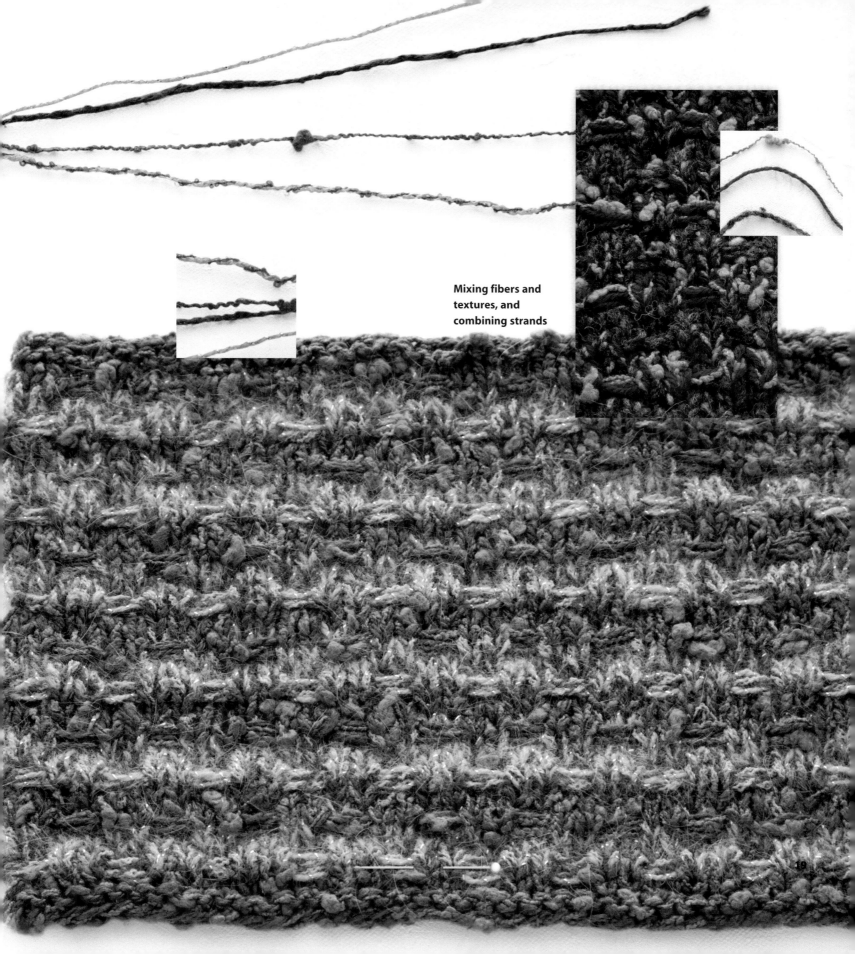

Mixing fibers and textures, and combining strands

19

2-COLOR TEXTURE, page 68

Because I've never seen this knit in 1 color, I swatched to see what it looks like in blue wool. What a pleasant surprise! In 1 color, it is wonderful.

Off to my stash for more play. First I held the blue wool together with a strand of matching mohair and used 2 strands of hand-dyed silk for the second color. How about brown knitting worsted and a rayon slub held with mohair yarn? It's hard to stop blending yarns this way! Next I held red wool with brown mohair as 1 color, and a red rayon bouclé with mustard Shetland wool as the second color. Switching my swatching to shades of gray and red, I used the yarns from page 19 for a very couture-looking fabric.

As you can see, the sky's the limit. This stitch pattern is remarkable!

Original in 2 colors

Worked in 1 color

stitches for TAILORED knits

Reduce value contrast and mix fibers and
textures, and combine 2 strands for each yarn

21

Diagonal Fabrics

The most basic woven fabric is *plain weave*, in which the horizontal thread (the weft) weaves *over* the first vertical thread (the warp) then *under* the second—a 2-thread repeat. In the next row, the weft goes *under* the first warp thread and *over* the second. In knitters' terms, plain weave is a 2-stitch, 2-row repeat.

The simplest diagonal weave involves a repeat of 3 warps, and is known as *twill*. The first weft goes *over* 1 and *under* 2. For each subsequent weft, the over-1-under-2 sequence shifts to the left or right 1 warp thread, repeating every 3 rows. In the top row of photos, you see more of the lighter warp threads than the darker weft threads, so this is a warp-faced twill. On the other side of the fabric, the sequence is *over* 2 and *under* 1, and the fabric is weft-faced.

In the second row, you see an over-2-under-2 twill. This 4-thread sequence repeats every 4 rows. The diagonal of this balanced weave (equal amounts of warp and weft show on the surface of the fabric) can move to the left or the right.

In the third row, you see a chevron weave, which combines left and right diagonals across the width of the fabric.

In the color photos at right, knitting builds the diagonals with knits and purls, lace units, slipped stitches, cables, and 2-color knitting.

Charts and instructions are given for both left-leaning and right-leaning diagonals. In all cases but one, rearranging the order of the rows is all it takes to create these mirrored diagonals. For Diagonal Lace on page 24, we substitute a right-leaning decrease (k2tog) and rewrite the pattern for the right slant, working the lace unit as [yarn over, k2tog] instead of a [SSK, yarn over].

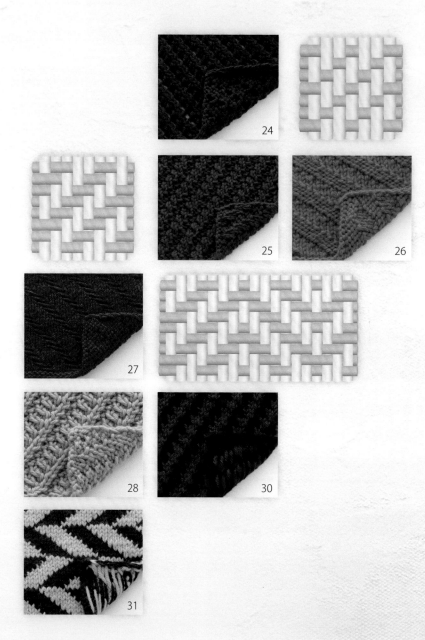

24

25

26

27

28

30

31

stitches for TAILORED knits

Diagonal Rib

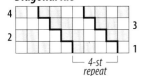

Stitch key

☐ Knit on RS, purl on WS

☐ Purl on RS, knit on WS

Reverse Diagonal Rib

The diagonal line of rib travels from lower right to upper left on RS of fabric, from lower left to upper right on WS of fabric. You can also reverse the diagonal by working the rows in reverse order: 4, 3, 2, 1.

MULTIPLE OF 4 + 2 EDGE STITCHES

Cast on and knit 1 row.

Row 1 (RS) K1, **[k2, p2]** to last stitch, k1.

Row 2 **[K2, p2]** to last 2 stitches, k2.

Row 3 K1, p2, **[k2, p2]** to last 3 stitches, k3.

Row 4 K1, p1, **[k2, p2]** to last 4 stitches, k2, p1, k1.

Repeat Rows 1–4.

WS

RS

Diagonal Lace

MULTIPLE OF 3 + 2 + 2 EDGE STITCHES

SKP
Slip 1 knitwise, k1, pass slipped stitch over knit stitch.

Cast on and knit 1 row.
Row 1 (RS) K3, **[yo, SKP, k1]** to last stitch, k1.
Rows 2, 4, 6 K1, purl to last stitch, k1.
Row 3 K1, **[yo, SKP, k1]** to end.
Row 5 K2, **[yo, SKP, k1]** to last 2 stitches, k2.
Repeat Rows 1–6.

For Reverse Diagonal, work Rows 1, 3, and 5 as follows:
Row 1 (RS) K2, **[k2tog, yo, k1]** to last 2 stitches, k2.
Row 3 (RS) K1, **[k2tog, yo, k1]** to end.
Row 5 (RS) K3, **[k2tog, yo, k1]** to last stitch, k1.

Diagonal Lace

└ 3-st ┘
repeat

Reverse Diagonal Lace

└ 3-st ┘
repeat

Stitch key

☐	Knit on RS, purl on WS
▓	Purl on RS, knit on WS
O	Yo
\	SKP
/	K2tog

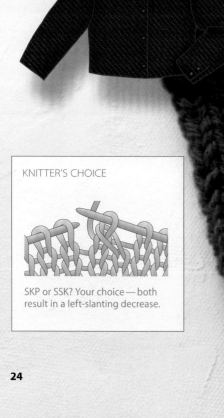

KNITTER'S CHOICE

SKP or SSK? Your choice — both result in a left-slanting decrease.

2-by-2 Diagonal Rib

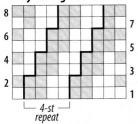

8
7
6
5
4
3
2
1

4-st repeat

Reverse 2-by-2 Diagonal Rib

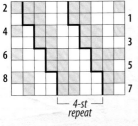

2
1
4
3
6
5
8
7

4-st repeat

RS

The WS of the fabric looks identical to the RS except the diagonal line is reversed. You can also reverse the diagonal by working the rows in 7, 8, 5, 6, 3, 4, 1, 2 order.

MULTIPLE OF 4 + 2 EDGE STITCHES

Cast on and knit 1 row.

Row 1 (RS) K1, **[k2, p2]** to last stitch, k1.

Rows 2, 4, 6, 8 K1, knit the knits and purl the purls to last stitch, k1.

Row 3 **[K2, p2]** to last 2 stitches, k2.

Row 5 K1, p2, **[k2, p2]** to last 3 stitches, k3.

Row 7 K1, p1, **[k2, p2]** to last 4 stitches, k2, p1, k1.

Repeat Rows 1–8.

WS

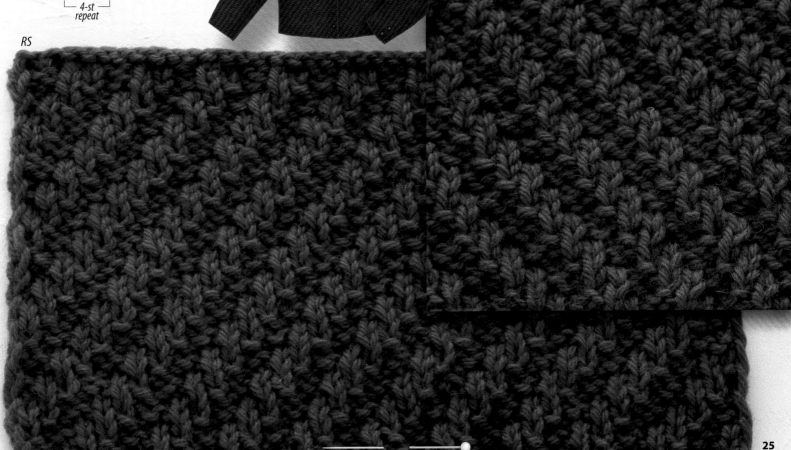

K4-P4 Diagonal

MULTIPLE OF 8 + 2 EDGE STITCHES

Cast on and knit 1 row.
Row 1 (RS) K1, **[p4, k4]** to last stitch, k1.
Row 2 K1, p3, **[k4, p4]** to last 6 stitches, k4, p1, k1.
Row 3 K3, **[p4, k4]** to last 7 stitches, p4, k3.
Row 4 K1, p1, **[k4, p4]** to last 8 stitches, k4, p3, k1.
Row 5 K1, **[k4, p4]** to last stitch, k1.
Row 6 **[K4, p4]** to last 2 stitches, k2.
Row 7 K1, p2, **[k4, p4]** to last 7 stitches, k4, p2, k1.
Row 8 K2, **[p4, k4]** to end.
Repeat Rows 1–8.

K4-P4 Diagonal

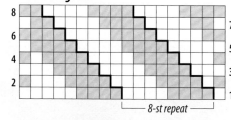

8-st repeat

Reverse K4-P4 Diagonal

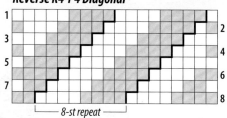

8-st repeat

Stitch key

☐ Knit on RS, purl on WS
▨ Purl on RS, knit on WS

The WS of the fabric looks identical to the RS except the diagonal line is reversed. You can also reverse the diagonal by working the rows in reverse order: 8, 7, 6, 5, 4, 3, 2, 1. Since this turns even-numbered WS rows into RS rows and vice versa, work from chart only.

RS

WS

stitches for TAILORED knits

Woven Diagonal

Woven Diagonal Herringbone

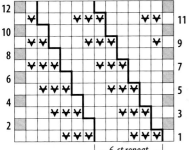

Reverse Woven Diagonal Herringbone

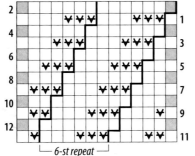

6-st repeat

The diagonal line is reversed on the WS of the fabric.
You can also reverse the diagonal by working the
rows in 11, 12, 9, 10, 7, 8, 5, 6, 3, 4, 1, 2 order.

MULTIPLE OF 6 + 2 EDGE STITCHES

SL
Slip purlwise with yarn at RS of work.

Cast on and knit 1 row.
Row 1 (RS) K1, **[sl 3, k3]** to last stitch, k1.
Rows 2, 4, 6, 8, 10, 12 K1, purl to last stitch, k1.
Row 3 K2, **[sl 3, k3]** to end.
Row 5 K3, **[sl 3, k3]** to last 5 stitches, sl 3, k2.
Row 7 K4, **[sl 3, k3]** to last 4 stitches, sl 3, k1.
Row 9 K1, sl 1, k3, **[sl 3, k3]** to last 3 stitches, sl 2, k1.
Row 11 K1, sl 2, k3, **[sl 3, k3]** to last 2 stitches, sl 1, k1.
Repeat Rows 1–12.

RS

WS

27

Relief Diagonal

MULTIPLE OF 6 + 2 EDGE STITCHES

Cast on and knit 1 row.

Row 1 (RS) K1, p1, 1/1 RC, 1/1 LC, **[p2, 1/1 RC, 1/1 LC]** to last 2 stitches, p1, k1.

Rows 2, 4, 6, 8, 10, 12 K1, knit the knits and purl the purls to last stitch, k1.

Row 3 K1, 1/1 RC, 1/1 LC, **[p2, 1/1 RC, 1/1 LC]** to last 3 stitches, p2, k1.

Row 5 K2, 1/1 LC, **[p2, 1/1 RC, 1/1 LC]** to last 4 stitches, p2, k2.

Row 7 K1, 1/1 LC, **[p2, 1/1 RC, 1/1 LC]** to last 5 stitches, p2, 1/1 RC, k1.

Row 9 K2, **[p2, 1/1 RC, 1/1 LC]** to last 6 stitches, p2, 1/1 RC, k2.

Row 11 K1, **[p2, 1/1 RC, 1/1 LC]** to last stitch, k1.

Repeat Rows 1–12.

Relief Diagonal

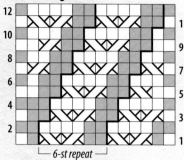

└─ 6-st repeat ─┘

Reverse Relief Diagonal

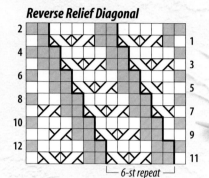

└─ 6-st repeat ─┘

RS

Stitch key

☐ Knit on RS, purl on WS

▨ Purl on RS, knit on WS

⧄ **1/1 RC**

⧅ **1/1 LC**

1/1 RC (1/1 RIGHT CROSS)

1 Bring right needle *in front of* first stitch on left needle. Knit second stitch but *do not remove* it from left needle.

2 Knit first stitch.

3 Pull both stitches off left needle.

Completed 1/1 RC: 1 stitch crosses over 1 stitch and to the right.

1/1 LC (1/1 LEFT CROSS)

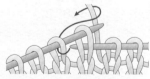

1 Bring right needle *behind* first stitch on left needle, and *to front between* first and second stitches. Knit second stitch, but *do not remove* it from left needle.

2 Bring right needle to right and in front of first stitch, then knit first stitch.

3 Pull both stitches off left needle. Completed 1/1 LC: 1 stitch crosses over 1 stitch and to the left.

The diagonal line is reversed on the WS of the fabric. You can also reverse the diagonal by working the rows in 11, 12, 9, 10, 7, 8, 5, 6, 3, 4, 1, 2 order.

KNITTER'S CHOICE

The 1/1 RC and 1/1 LC can also be worked using a cable needle:

Slip 1 to cable needle

AND
hold to back for 1/1 RC

OR
hold to front for 1/1 LC

THEN
k1; k1 from cable needle.

WS

2-color Diagonal

MULTIPLE OF 4 + 2 EDGE STITCHES
*Worked in stranded knitting with 2
colors: A (Black) and B (Brown).*

With A, cast on and knit 1 row.
Row 1 and all RS rows Working in colors shown on
chart, knit.
Row 2 and all WS rows Working in colors shown on
chart, k1, purl to last stitch, k1.
Repeat Rows 1–8.

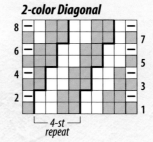

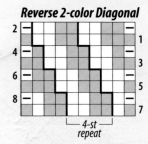

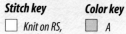

*The diagonal line is reversed on
the WS of the fabric. You can also
reverse the diagonal by working
the rows in 7, 8, 5, 6, 3, 4, 1, 2 order.*

Stitch key

▢ Knit on RS,
purl on WS

▬ Knit on WS

Color key

▨ A

▢ B

Arrowhead

Arrowhead

MULTIPLE OF 10 + 2 EDGE STITCHES
Worked in stranded knitting with 2 colors: A (Black) and B (Gray).

With A, cast on and knit 1 row.
Row 1 and all RS rows Working in colors shown on chart, knit.
Row 2 and all WS rows Working in colors shown on chart, k1, purl to last stitch, k1.
Repeat Rows 1–16.

For 1-color Arrowhead, follow chart using Knit/Purl key.

— 10-st repeat —

Stitch key

☐ Knit on RS, purl on WS

— Knit on WS

Color key

☐ A

☐ B

Knit/Purl key

☐ Knit on RS, purl on WS

☐ Purl on RS, knit on WS

31

Basketweave Fabrics

Another basic woven structure is basketweave. Here, the horizontal thread goes *over* 2 and *under* 2 — the same pairs of threads — twice, then alternates to go *under* and *over* the pairs twice for a 4-thread, 4-row repeat. This alternating structure is really a scaled-up plain weave, named for its resemblance to baskets woven of flat materials.

Knitting can simulate the lattice appearance of basketweave in several ways: in knits and purls, cables, slipped stitches with the yarn on the right side of the fabric, and color.

Perhaps the most interesting stitches in this section turn basketweave on an angle: Cabled Basketweave on page 35 and Diagonal Basket on page 40. Mosaic Basketweave on page 41 uses 2 colors and slipped stitches to create the trompe l'oeil.

stitches for TAILORED knits

Irish Basketweave

Irish Basketweave

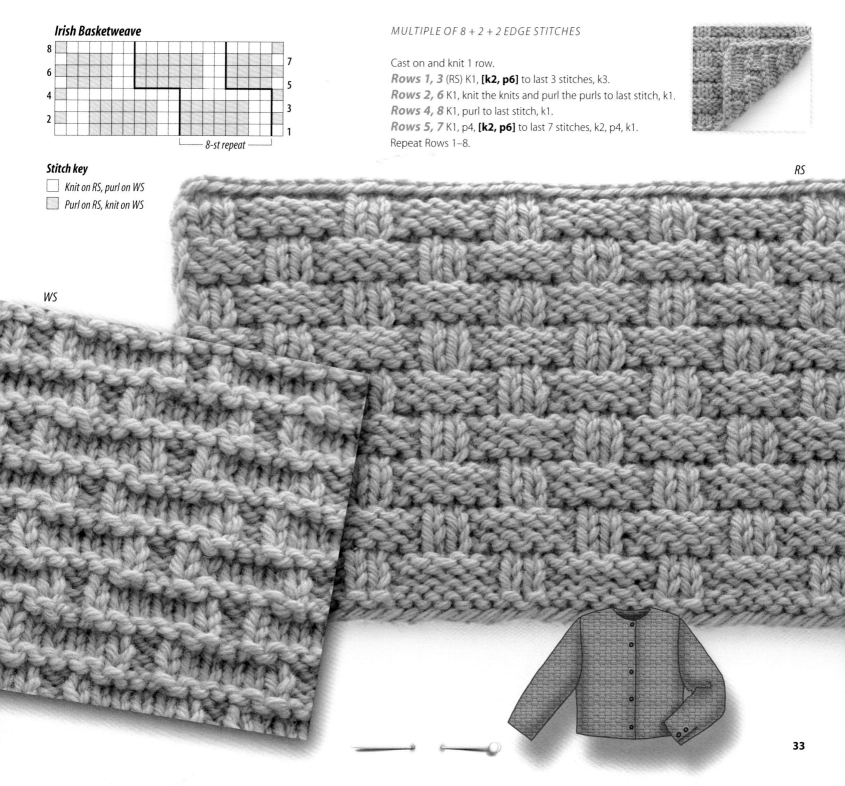

8
6
4
2

8-st repeat

7
5
3
1

Stitch key

☐ Knit on RS, purl on WS

▨ Purl on RS, knit on WS

MULTIPLE OF 8 + 2 + 2 EDGE STITCHES

Cast on and knit 1 row.
Rows 1, 3 (RS) K1, **[k2, p6]** to last 3 stitches, k3.
Rows 2, 6 K1, knit the knits and purl the purls to last stitch, k1.
Rows 4, 8 K1, purl to last stitch, k1.
Rows 5, 7 K1, p4, **[k2, p6]** to last 7 stitches, k2, p4, k1.
Repeat Rows 1–8.

RS

WS

33

Woven Basketweave

MULTIPLE OF 4 + 2 + 2 EDGE STITCHES

Cast on and knit 1 row.
Row 1 (RS) Knit.
Rows 2, 6 K1, purl to last stitch, k1.
Rows 3, 8 K1, k2, **[p2, k2]** to last stitch, k1.
Rows 4, 7 K1, **[p2, k2]** to last 3 stitches, p2, k1.
Row 5 Knit.
Repeat Rows 1–8.

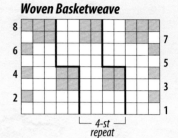

Woven Basketweave

4-st repeat

RS

WS

stitches for TAILORED knits

Cabled Basketweave

Cabled Basketweave

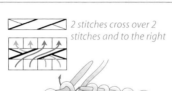

4
3
2
1

|— 4-st repeat —|

Stitch key

☐ Knit on RS, purl on WS

▨ Knit on WS

◪ 2/2 RC

◪ 2/2 LC

MULTIPLE OF 4 + 2 EDGE STITCHES

Cast on and knit 1 row.

Row 1 (RS) K1, **[2/2 LC]** to last stitch, k1.

Rows 2, 4 K1, purl to last stitch, k1.

Row 3 K1, k2, **[2/2 RC]** to last 3 stitches, k2, k1.

Repeat Rows 1–4.

2/2 RC (2/2 RIGHT CROSS)

2 stitches cross over 2 stitches and to the right

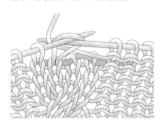

1 Slip 2 stitches onto a cable needle and hold (let it hang) to *back* of the knitting. Knit the next 2 stitches from the left needle.

2 Then, holding the cable needle in your left hand, knit the 2 stitches from the cable needle.

2/2 LC (2/2 LEFT CROSS)

2 stitches cross over 2 stitches and to the left

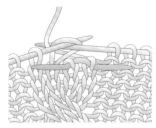

1 Slip 2 stitches onto a cable needle and hold (let it hang) to *front* of the knitting. Knit the next 2 stitches from the left needle.

2 Then, holding the cable needle in your left hand, knit the 2 stitches from the cable needle.

Slip-stitch Basketweave

MULTIPLE OF 4 + 2 EDGE STITCHES

SL
Slip purlwise with yarn at RS of work.

Cast on and knit 1 row.
Rows 1, 2 K1, **[k2, p2]** to last stitch, k1.
Row 3 (RS) K1, **[k2, sl 2]** to last stitch, k1.
Row 4 K1, **[sl 2, p2]** to last stitch, k1.
Rows 5, 6 K1, **[p2, k2]** to last stitch, k1.
Row 7 K1, **[sl 2, k2]** to last stitch, k1.
Row 8 K1, **[p2, sl 2]** to last stitch, k1.
Repeat Rows 1–8.

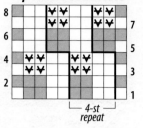

Slip-stitch Basketweave

4-st repeat

RS

WS

stitches for TAILORED *knits*

Half Linen Stitch

Half Linen Stitch

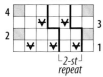

└ 2-st ┘
repeat

Stitch key

☐ Knit on RS, purl on WS

▨ Knit on WS

❤ Slip purlwise with yarn at RS of work

MULTIPLE OF 2 + 1 + 2 EDGE STITCHES

SL

Slip purlwise with yarn at RS of work.

Cast on and knit 1 row.
Row 1 (RS) K1, **[sl 1, k1]** to end.
Rows 2, 4 K1, purl to last stitch, k1.
Row 3 K2, **[sl 1, k1]** to last stitch, k1.
Repeat Rows 1–4.

Stranded Basketweave

MULTIPLE OF 6 + 3 + 2 EDGE STITCHES

SL

Slip purlwise with yarn at RS of work.

Cast on and knit 1 row.

Rows 1, 3 (RS) K4, **[p1, k1, p1, k3]** to last stitch, k1.

Rows 2, 4 K1, **[sl 3, k1, p1, k1]** to last 4 stitches, sl 3, k1.

Rows 5, 7 K1, **[p1, k1, p1, k3]** to last 4 stitches, **[p1, k1]** twice.

Rows 6, 8 K2, p1, k1, **[sl 3, k1, p1, k1]** to last stitch, k1.

Repeat Rows 1–8.

Stranded Basketweave

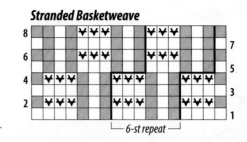

6-st repeat

Stitch key

- ☐ Knit on RS, purl on WS
- ▨ Purl on RS, knit on WS
- ⱴ Slip purlwise with yarn at RS of work

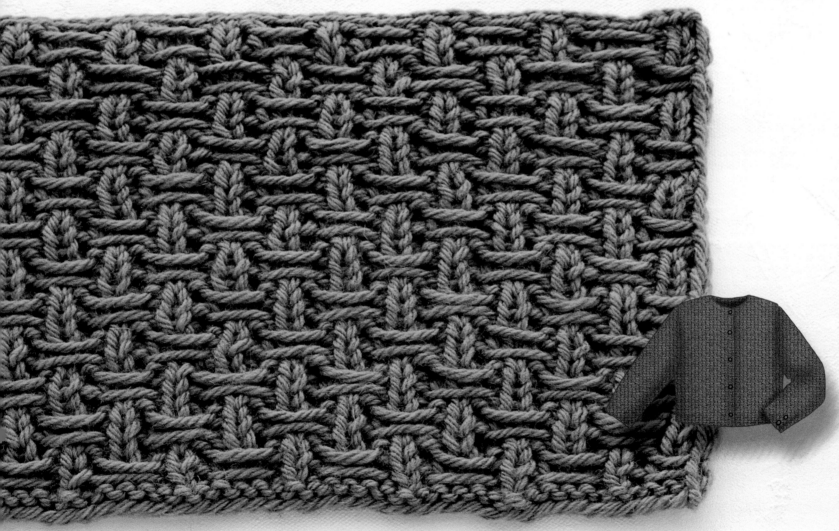

stitches for TAILORED knits

Ladder Basketweave

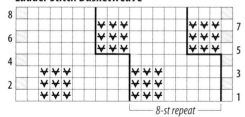

Ladder Stitch Basketweave

8-st repeat

MULTIPLE OF 8 + 1 + 2 EDGE STITCHES

SL

Slip purlwise with yarn at RS of work.

Cast on and knit 1 row.

Rows 1, 3 (RS) K1, **[k5, sl 3]** to last 2 stitches, k2.

Row 2 K1, p1, **[sl 3, p5]** to last stitch, k1.

Rows 4, 8 K1, purl to last stitch, k1.

Rows 5, 7 K1, **[sl 3, k5]** to last 2 stitches, k2.

Row 6 K1, p1, **[p5, sl 3]** to last stitch, k1.

Repeat Rows 1–8.

Diagonal Basket

MULTIPLE OF 4 + 3 + 2 EDGE STITCHES

SL
Slip purlwise with yarn at WS of work.

1/2 LC
Slip 1 to cable needle, hold to front, k2; k1 from cable needle.

1/2 RC
Slip 2 to cable needle, hold to back, k1; k2 from cable needle.

Cast on and knit 1 row.
Row 1 (RS) K1, **[sl 1, k3]** to end.
Row 2 K1, p2, **[sl 1, p3]** to last 2 stitches, sl 1, k1.
Row 3 K1, **[1/2 LC, k1]** to end.
Rows 4, 8 K1, purl to last stitch, k1.
Row 5 K5, **[sl 1, k3]** to end.
Row 6 K1, p2, **[sl 1, p3]** to last 2 stitches, p1, k1.
Row 7 K3, **[1/2 RC, k1]** to last 2 stitches, k2.
Repeat Rows 1–8.

For 2-color version, cast on and knit 1 row with A (Black). Change to B (Cranberry) and knit 1 row, purl 1 row. Work Rows 1–8, changing color at the beginning of every RS row.

Diagonal Basket

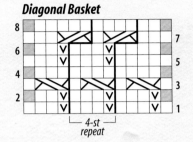

4-st repeat

Stitch key

☐ Knit on RS, purl on WS
▨ Knit on WS
V Slip purlwise with yarn at WS of work
⧄ 1/2 RC
⧅ 1/2 LC

Mosaic Basketweave

Mosaic Basketweave

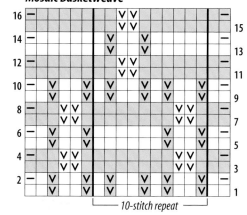

Stitch key

- ☐ Knit on RS, purl on WS
- ☐ Knit on WS
- ☑ Slip with yarn at WS of work

Color key

- ☐ A
- ☐ B

10-stitch repeat

MULTIPLE OF 10 + 6 + 2 EDGE STITCHES
Worked with 2 colors: A (Pink) and B (Navy).

SL
Slip purlwise with yarn at WS of work.

With B, cast on and knit 1 row.
Rows 1, 9 (RS) With A, k2, **[sl 1, k2, sl 1, k1]** to last 6 stitches, **[sl 1, k2]** twice.
Rows 2, 10 With A, k1, p1, sl 1, p2, **[sl 1, p1, sl 1, p2]** to last 3 stitches, sl 1, p1, k1.
Rows 3, 7 With B, k3, **[sl 2, k8]** to last 5 stitches, sl 2, k3.
Rows 4, 8 With B, k1, p2, **[sl 2, p8]** to last 5 stitches, sl 2, p2, k1.
Row 5 With A, k2, **[sl 1, k2, sl 1, k6]** to last 6 stitches, **[sl 1, k2]** twice.

Row 6 With A, k1, p1, sl 1, p2, **[sl 1, p6, sl 1, p2]** to last 3 stitches, sl 1, p1, k1.
Rows 11, 15 With B, k8, **[sl 2, k8]** to end.
Rows 12, 16 With B, k1, p7, **[sl 2, p8]** to last 10 stitches, sl 2, p7, k1.
Row 13 With A, k7, **[sl 1, k2, sl 1, k6]** to last stitch, k1.
Row 14 With A, k1, p6, **[sl 1, p2, sl1, p6]** to last stitch, k1.
Repeat Rows 1–16.

41

Houndstooth Fabrics

Houndstooth is one of the most popular woven fabrics. It appears and reappears in fashion collections. Our drawing shows 4 dark threads alternating with 4 light threads both horizontally and vertically. The weave structure, a 2/2 twill (page 22), produces a small check with four points.

Why such a strange name for a fabric? It was often used in clothing for sportsmen, and it is speculated that hunters thought the pointed squares resembled their hounds' molars.

Coco Chanel first used the fabric in her 1936 collection. In the sixties, Anne Klein, Geoffrey Beene, and others began using it.

Houndstooth adapts beautifully to knitting. It can be produced in a garter-stitch fabric by knitting 2 rows in dark wool and 2 rows in light, slipping stitches to make the pattern appear. It can be made larger by slipping more stitches. It can be worked in stockinette. In 2-color stranded knitting (using 2 colors in each row), the classic shape appears more clearly. The larger interpretations on pages 48 and 49 are similar to those recently seen on the runways. Slipped stitches produce the points in the patterns on pages 50 and 51. They are really fun to knit and produce wonderfully interesting fabrics.

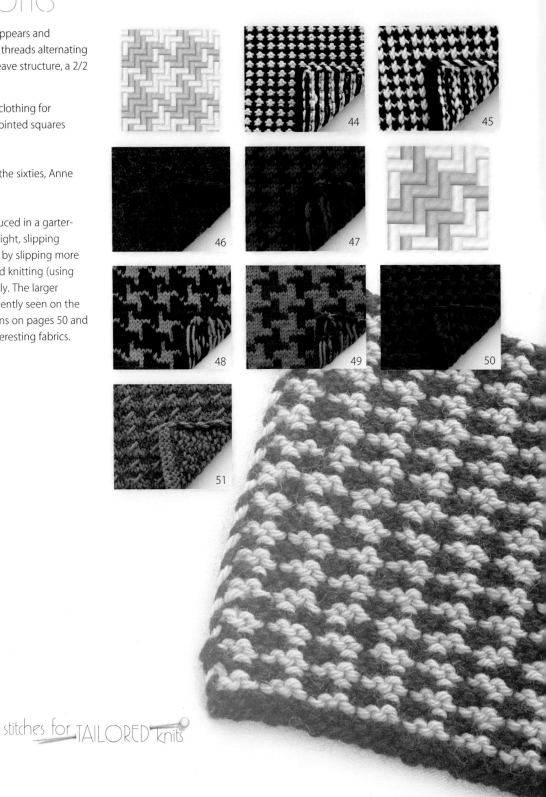

stitches for TAILORED knits

Small Houndstooth

In Stockinette

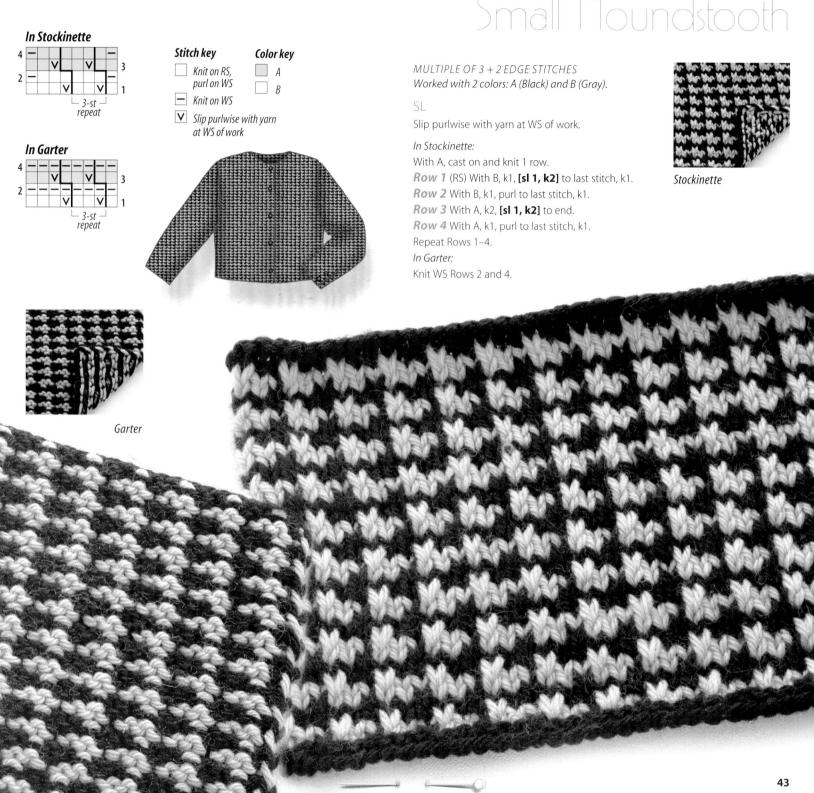

Stitch key

☐ Knit on RS, purl on WS

— Knit on WS

Ⅴ Slip purlwise with yarn at WS of work

Color key

▨ A

☐ B

In Garter

MULTIPLE OF 3 + 2 EDGE STITCHES
Worked with 2 colors: A (Black) and B (Gray).

SL
Slip purlwise with yarn at WS of work.

In Stockinette:
With A, cast on and knit 1 row.
Row 1 (RS) With B, k1, **[sl 1, k2]** to last stitch, k1.
Row 2 With B, k1, purl to last stitch, k1.
Row 3 With A, k2, **[sl 1, k2]** to end.
Row 4 With A, k1, purl to last stitch, k1.
Repeat Rows 1–4.
In Garter:
Knit WS Rows 2 and 4.

Stockinette

Garter

Tiny Houndstooth

MULTIPLE OF 2 + 1 + 2 EDGE STITCHES
Worked with 2 colors: A (Black) and B (White).

SL

Slip purlwise with yarn at WS of work.

With A, cast on and knit 1 row.
Row 1 (RS) With B, k1, **[sl 1, k1]** to end.
Row 2 With B, knit.
Row 3 With A, k2, **[sl 1, k1]** to last stitch, k1.
Row 4 With A, knit.
Repeat Rows 1–4.

In Garter

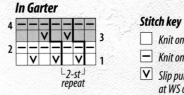

Stitch key

	Knit on RS, purl on WS
—	Knit on WS
V	Slip purlwise with yarn at WS of work
Ⓠ	K1 tbl

Color key

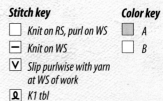

| A |
| B |

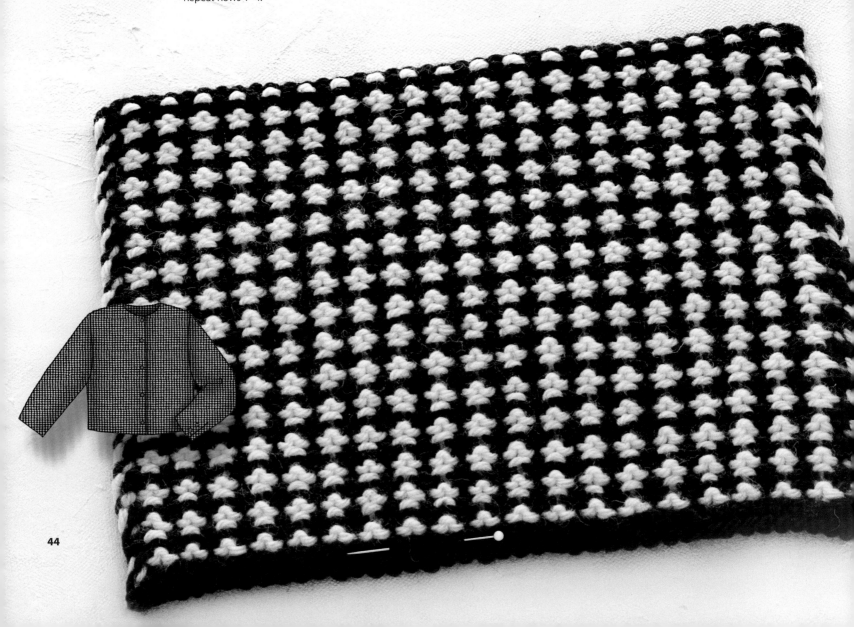

In Stockinette

4	—	ꝏ	V	ꝏ	V	—	
2	—	V	ꝏ	V	ꝏ	—	3
		V	ꝏ	V	ꝏ		1

⎣2-st⎦
repeat

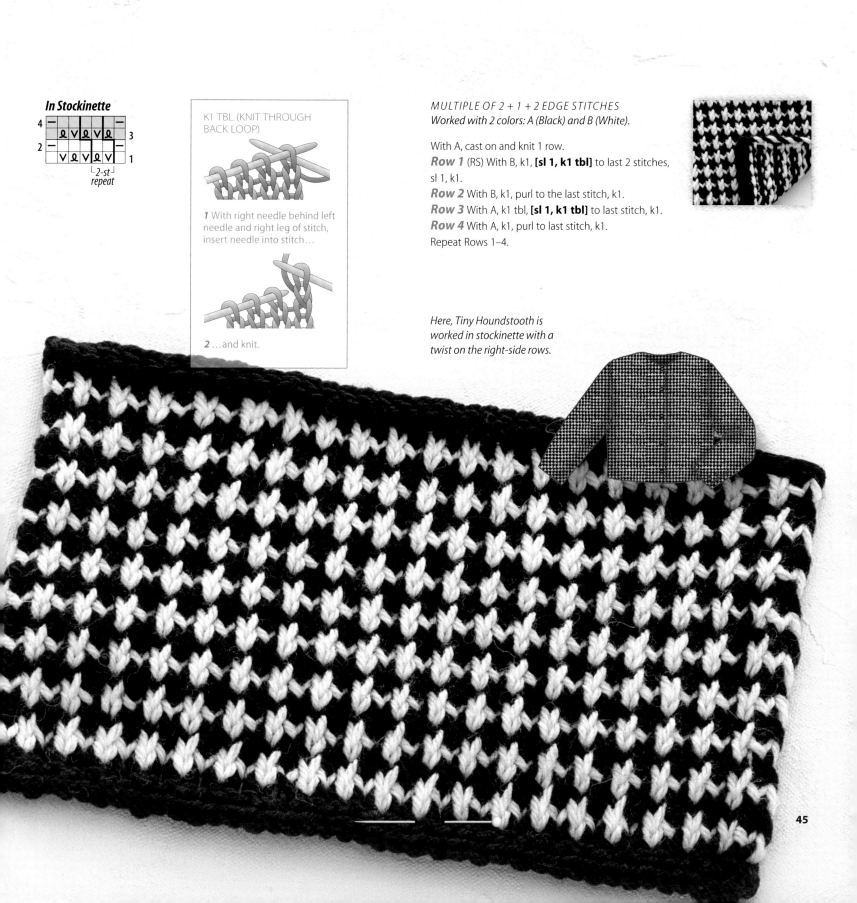

K1 TBL (KNIT THROUGH BACK LOOP)

1 With right needle behind left needle and right leg of stitch, insert needle into stitch…

2 …and knit.

MULTIPLE OF 2 + 1 + 2 EDGE STITCHES
Worked with 2 colors: A (Black) and B (White).

With A, cast on and knit 1 row.
Row 1 (RS) With B, k1, **[sl 1, k1 tbl]** to last 2 stitches, sl 1, k1.
Row 2 With B, k1, purl to the last stitch, k1.
Row 3 With A, k1 tbl, **[sl 1, k1 tbl]** to last stitch, k1.
Row 4 With A, k1, purl to last stitch, k1.
Repeat Rows 1–4.

Here, Tiny Houndstooth is worked in stockinette with a twist on the right-side rows.

45

Big Houndstooth 2 Ways

MULTIPLE OF 4 + 2 EDGE STITCHES
Worked with 2 colors: A (Red) and B (Gray).

With A, cast on and knit 1 row.
Rows 1, 3 (RS) Knit in colors shown on chart.
Rows 2, 4 Working in colors shown on chart, k1, purl to last stitch, k1.
Repeat Rows 1–4.

Version 1

4-st repeat
4-row repeat

Stitch key
☐ Knit on RS, purl on WS
— Knit on WS

Color key
☐ A
▨ B

Version 2

Worked with 2 colors, A (Black) and B (Blue).
Rows 2 and 3 are the same for both versions,
but switching Rows 1 and 4 changes the
shape of the tooth for Versions 1 and 2.

4

2

4-st
repeat

3

1

4-row
repeat

Diamond Houndstooth

MULTIPLE OF 7 + 2 EDGE STITCHES
Worked with 2 colors: A (Black) and B (Tan).

With A, cast on and knit 1 row.
Row 1 and all RS rows Knit in colors shown on chart.
Row 2 and all WS rows Working in colors shown on chart, k1, purl to last stitch, k1.
Repeat Rows 1–14.

Diamond Houndstooth

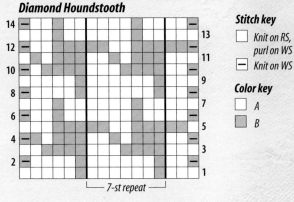

14 — 13
12 — 11
10 — 9
8 — 7
6 — 5
4 — 3
2 — 1

⌞— 7-st repeat —⌟

Stitch key
◻ Knit on RS, purl on WS
— Knit on WS

Color key
◻ A
▨ B

This color pattern is really a 7-row repeat. If worked circularly, the chart would only consist of 7 rows. When worked back and forth, the first 7-row repeat begins with a RS row, the second with a WS row, and the chart is made up of 14 rows as shown.

Giant Houndstooth

Giant Houndstooth

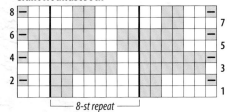

8-st repeat

MULTIPLE OF 8 + 2 EDGE STITCHES
Worked with 2 colors: A (Brown) and B (Tan).

With A, cast on and knit 1 row.
Row 1 and all RS rows Knit in colors shown on chart.
Row 2 and all WS rows Working in colors shown on chart, k1, purl to last stitch, k1.
Repeat Rows 1–8.

Fancy Slip Houndstooth

MULTIPLE OF 3 + 1 + 2 EDGE STITCHES
Worked with 2 colors: A (Black) and B (Red).

SL
Slip purlwise with yarn at WS.

With A, cast on, knit 2 rows, and purl 1 row.
Row 1 (RS) With B, k2, **[Fancy Slip]** to last stitch, k1.
Row 2 With B, k1, purl all stitches in order
(the B knit, A slip, and A yo) to last stitch, k1.
Row 3 With A, k1, **[Fancy Slip]** to last 2 stitches, k2.
Row 4 With A, k1, purl all stitches in order
(the A knit, B slip, and A yo), to last stitch, k1.
Repeat Rows 1–4.

FANCY SLIP

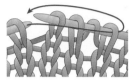

1 Slip 1 to right needle, yarn over, slip 1, knit 1.
2 Pass first slipped stitch over the following stitches and off the needle.

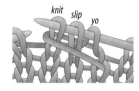

knit   slip   yo

Watch the order of stitches as you work the next row (work the knit stitch, then the slipped stitch, then the yo).

Fancy Slip Houndstooth

└─3-st─┘
repeat

Stitch key
☐ Knit on RS, purl on WS
− Knit on WS
╱ Fancy Slip
╱ 1/1 RSC

Color key
▨ A
☐ B

Houndstooth Check

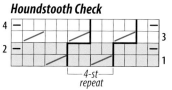

4-st repeat

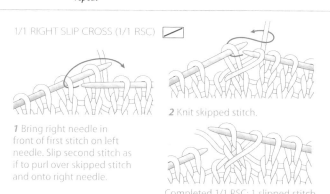

1/1 RIGHT SLIP CROSS (1/1 RSC)

1 Bring right needle in front of first stitch on left needle. Slip second stitch as if to purl over skipped stitch and onto right needle.

2 Knit skipped stitch.

Completed 1/1 RSC: 1 slipped stitch crosses around 1 stitch and to the right.

MULTIPLE OF 4 + 3 + 2 EDGE STITCHES
Worked with 2 colors: A (Tan) and B (Blue)

With A, cast on and knit 1 row.
Row 1 (RS) With A, k4, **[1/1 RSC, k2]** to last stitch, k1.
Row 2 With A, k1, purl to last stitch, k1.
Row 3 With B, k2, **[1/1 RSC, k2]** to last 3 stitches, 1/1 RST, k1.
Row 4 With B, k1, purl to last stitch, k1.
Repeat Rows 1–4.

Textured Fabrics

Here, the emphasis is on texture effects unique to knitting, with no attempt to mimic woven fabrics. The first pattern, Broken Rib, is yet another 4-stitch, 4-row repeat of just knits and purls. But isn't it crisp and effective?

Cluster, Knit Under, 3-to-1 increases and decreases, double wraps, cabling on right- and wrong-side rows — all these techniques add texture and visual interest to this intriguing group of fabrics.

And look at Speckle Rib, on page 58. It's a 2-stitch, 8-row repeat of knits, purls, and slips that gives endless opportunities to play with both yarn color and the pattern repeat.

54

55

56

57

58

59

60

stitches for TAILORED knits

Broken Rib

MULTIPLE OF 4 + 1 + 2 EDGE STITCHES

Cast on and knit 1 row.

Row 1 (RS) K2, **[p3, k1]** to last stitch, k1.

Rows 2, 4 K1, knit the knits and purl the purls to last stitch, k1.

Row 3 K1, p2, k1, **[p3, k1]** to last 3 stitches, p2, k1.

Repeat Rows 1–4.

Broken Rib

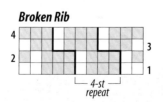

4

2

3

1

└ 4-st ┘
repeat

Cluster Stitch

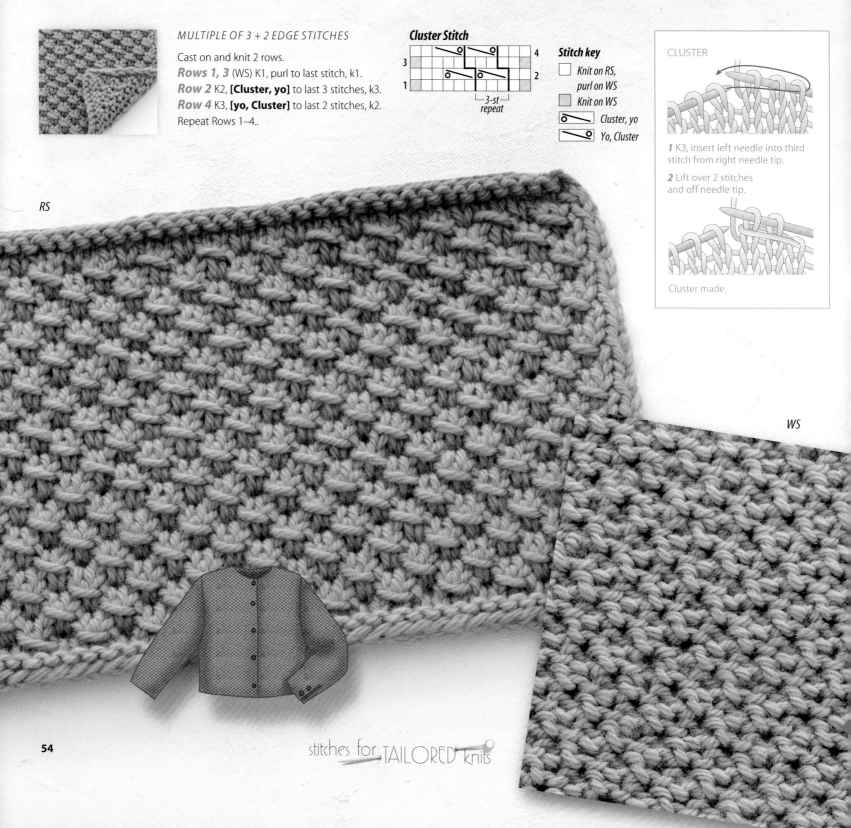

MULTIPLE OF 3 + 2 EDGE STITCHES

Cast on and knit 2 rows.
Rows 1, 3 (WS) K1, purl to last stitch, k1.
Row 2 K2, **[Cluster, yo]** to last 3 stitches, k3.
Row 4 K3, **[yo, Cluster]** to last 2 stitches, k2.
Repeat Rows 1–4..

Cluster Stitch

3
1
4
2

└─ 3-st ─┘
repeat

Stitch key

☐ Knit on RS, purl on WS

▨ Knit on WS

⬭╱ Cluster, yo

╱ Yo, Cluster

CLUSTER

1 K3, insert left needle into third stitch from right needle tip.

2 Lift over 2 stitches and off needle tip.

Cluster made.

RS

WS

54

stitches for TAILORED knits

Pebbles

	4	K		K		
			/		/	3
	2					
						1

└ 2-st ┘
repeat

Stitch key

☐ Knit on RS, purl on WS

☐ Knit on WS

╱ K2tog

K Knit Under

■ Stitches do not exist in these areas of chart

KNIT UNDER

Knit under the strand before the next stitch.

MULTIPLE OF 2 + 2 EDGE STITCHES

Cast on and knit 1 row.

Row 1 (RS) Knit.

Row 2 K1, purl to last stitch, k1.

Row 3 K1, **[k2tog]** to last stitch, k1.

Row 4 K1, **[Knit Under, k1]** to last stitch, k1.

Repeat Rows 1–4.

Trinity Stitch

RS

WS

MULTIPLE OF 4 + 2 EDGE STITCHES

Cast on and knit 1 row.
Rows 1, 3 (RS) K1, purl to last stitch, k1.
Row 2 K1, **[k1-p1-k1 into next stitch, p3tog]** to last stitch, k1.
Row 4 K1, **[p3tog, k1-p1-k1 into next stitch]** to last stitch, k1.
Repeat Rows 1–4.

Trinity Stitch, named for its 1-to-3 increases and 3-to-1 decreases. Is also called Bramble Stitch.

Trinity Stitch

4	/3	V	/3	V	/3	V	/3	V
									3
2	V	/3	V	/3	V	/3	V	/3
									1

⌞— 4-st repeat —⌟

Stitch key

☐ Knit on RS, purl on WS

▨ Purl on RS, knit on WS

Ⅴ K1-p1-k1 into stitch

/3 P3tog

stitches for TAILORED knits

Brick Stitch

```
16  □V□□V□□V□
   V  V  V        15
14  V  V  V
   V  V  V        13
   ℋ  ℋ  ℋ
12  V  V  V
   V  V  V        11
10  V  V  V
   V  V  V
   ℋ  ℋ  ℋ         9
8  □□V□□V
   V  V           7
6  V  V
   V  V
   ℋ  ℋ           5
4  V  V
   V  V            3
2  V  V
   ℋ  ℋ            1
```

└ 4-st ┘
repeat

Small Brick

```
12  V  V  V
   V  V  V        11
10  V  V  V
   ℋ  ℋ  ℋ         9
   □V□□V
4  V  V            3
2  V  V
   ℋ  ℋ            1
```

└ 4-st ┘
repeat

This pattern can also be worked as an 8-row repeat, alternating Rows 1–4 with Rows 9–12.

Stitch key

□ Knit on RS, purl on WS

□ Knit on WS

V Slip purlwise with yarn at WS of work

ℋ Knit with double wrap

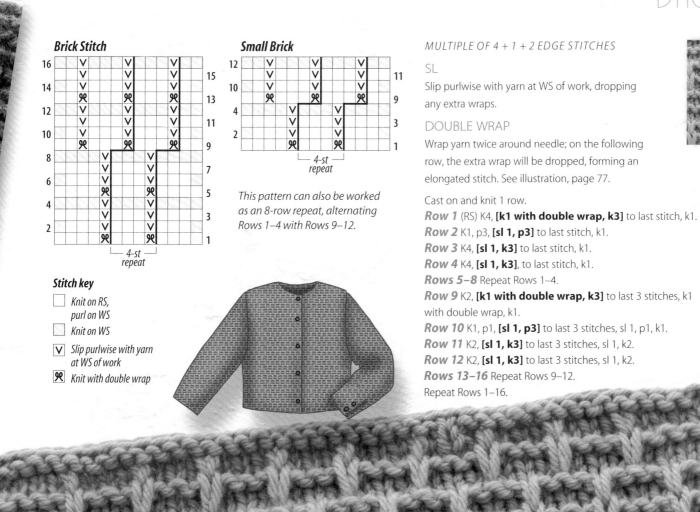

MULTIPLE OF 4 + 1 + 2 EDGE STITCHES

SL

Slip purlwise with yarn at WS of work, dropping any extra wraps.

DOUBLE WRAP

Wrap yarn twice around needle; on the following row, the extra wrap will be dropped, forming an elongated stitch. See illustration, page 77.

Cast on and knit 1 row.

Row 1 (RS) K4, **[k1 with double wrap, k3]** to last stitch, k1.

Row 2 K1, p3, **[sl 1, p3]** to last stitch, k1.

Row 3 K4, **[sl 1, k3]** to last stitch, k1.

Row 4 K4, **[sl 1, k3]**, to last stitch, k1.

Rows 5–8 Repeat Rows 1–4.

Row 9 K2, **[k1 with double wrap, k3]** to last 3 stitches, k1 with double wrap, k1.

Row 10 K1, p1, **[sl 1, p3]** to last 3 stitches, sl 1, p1, k1.

Row 11 K2, **[sl 1, k3]** to last 3 stitches, sl 1, k2.

Row 12 K2, **[sl 1, k3]** to last 3 stitches, sl 1, k2.

Rows 13–16 Repeat Rows 9–12.

Repeat Rows 1–16.

Speckle Rib

MULTIPLE OF 2 + 1 + 2 EDGE STITCHES

SL
Slip purlwise with yarn at WS of work.

Cast on and knit 1 row.
Rows 1, 5 (RS) Knit.
Rows 2, 6 K1, purl to last stitch, k1.
Rows 3, 4 K1, **[sl 1, k1]** to end.
Rows 7, 8 K2, **[sl 1, k1]** to last stitch, k1.
Repeat Rows 1–8.

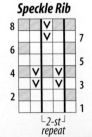

Speckle Rib

Stitch key

☐ Knit on RS, purl on WS

▨ ⊟ Knit on WS

Ⅴ Slip purlwise with yarn at WS of work

Color key

☐ A

▨ B

▨ C

2-st repeat

stitches for TAILORED knits

In 2 colors

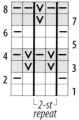

└ 2-st ┘ repeat

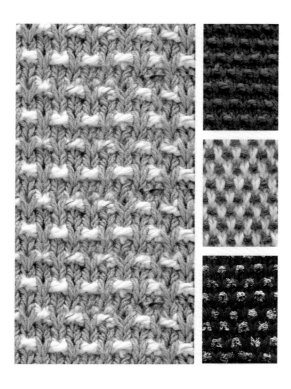

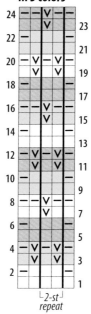

In 3 colors

└ 2-st ┘ repeat

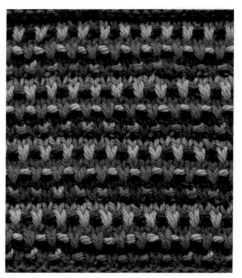

The 8-row stitch pattern requires 24 rows for the 3-color sequence to repeat.

In garter

└ 2-st ┘ repeat

Work as for Speckle Rib EXCEPT knit WS Rows 2 and 6.

Stacked

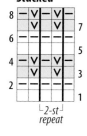

└ 2-st ┘ repeat

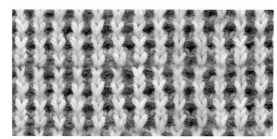

Work as for Speckle Rib EXCEPT repeat Rows 3 and 4 for Rows 7 and 8.

Double Stacks

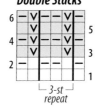

└ 3-st ┘ repeat

In this 6-row version, slip stitches are spaced 2 stitches apart and straddle 4 rows.

MULTIPLE OF 3 + 1 + EDGE STITCHES
Row 1 (RS) Knit.
Row 2 K1, purl to last stitch, k1.
Rows 3, 4, 5, 6 K1, **[sl1, k2]** to last 2 stitches, sl 1, k1.
Repeat Rows 1–6.

Twisted Texture

MULTIPLE OF 3 + 1 + 2 EDGE STITCHES

1/1 LC

Knit into back of second stitch, then knit first stitch and slip both stitches off left needle. See illustration, page 28.

Cast on and knit 2 rows.
Row 1 (WS) K1, purl to last stitch, k1.
Row 2 K1, p1, **[1/1 LC, p1]** to last stitch, k1.
Row 3 K2, **[1/1 RC, k1]** to last stitch, k1.
Row 4 Knit.
Repeat Rows 1–4.

Twisted Texture

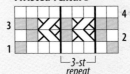

—3-st—
repeat

1/1 RC (1/1 RIGHT CROSS) WORKED ON WS ROW

1 Bring right needle *in front of* first stitch on left needle. Purl second stitch but *do not remove* it from left needle.

2 Purl first stitch.
3 Pull both stitches off left needle.

Completed 1/1 RC as seen on RS: 1 stitch crosses over 1 stitch and to the right.

stitches for TAILORED knits

English Tweed

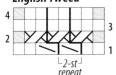

2-st repeat

Stitch key

- Knit on RS, purl on WS
- Purl on RS, knit on WS
- Sl 1, k1, yo, psso
- 1/1 RC
- 1/1 LC

SL 1, K1, YO, PSSO

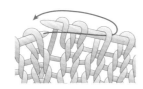

1 Slip 1 stitch to right needle, knit 1, yarn over.
2 Pass slipped stitch over both knit stitch and yarn-over.

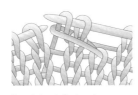

Result is a left-slanting slipped stitch

MULTIPLE OF 2 + 2 EDGE STITCHES

SL

Slip purlwise with yarn at WS of work.

Cast on and knit 1 row.
Row 1 (RS) K2, **[sl 1, k1, yo, psso]** to last 2 stitches, k2.
Row 2 K1, **[1/1 RC]** to last stitch, k1.
Row 3 Knit.
Row 4 K1, purl to last stitch, k1.
Repeat Rows 1–4.

Colored Fabrics

We have all discovered — sometimes the hard way — that colors don't mix in the same way in a stitch pattern as they do in skeins, balls, hanks, or even strands.

For relevant color exploration, all you need to do is to swatch, and this section is filled with patterns for you to color and re-color, again and again.

These stitches are good targets for some of the Change It Up! approaches from the front of the book. Our exploration of Garter Slip begins on page 16: 3-color swatches expand the 1- and 2-color versions shown here. You can compare the natural and bright palettes.

Then on pages 18–21, you can follow as we first remove a color for one swatch then mix fibers and textures, combining finer strands for both A and B. This results in a couple of spectacular blends for both 2-color Texture from page 68 and Slip-stitch Fabric from page 69.

The Mix it up! jacket on page 9 shows how combining different versions of one stitch pattern in a single garment can result in a unique knit.

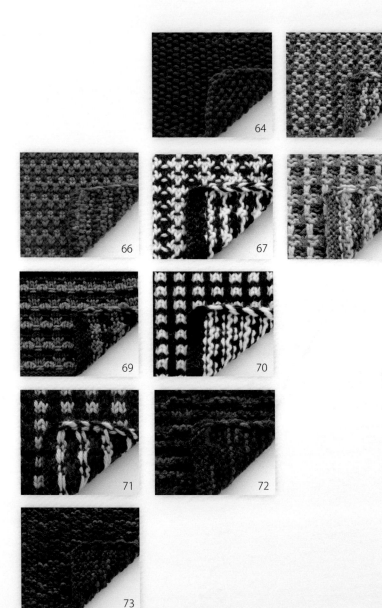

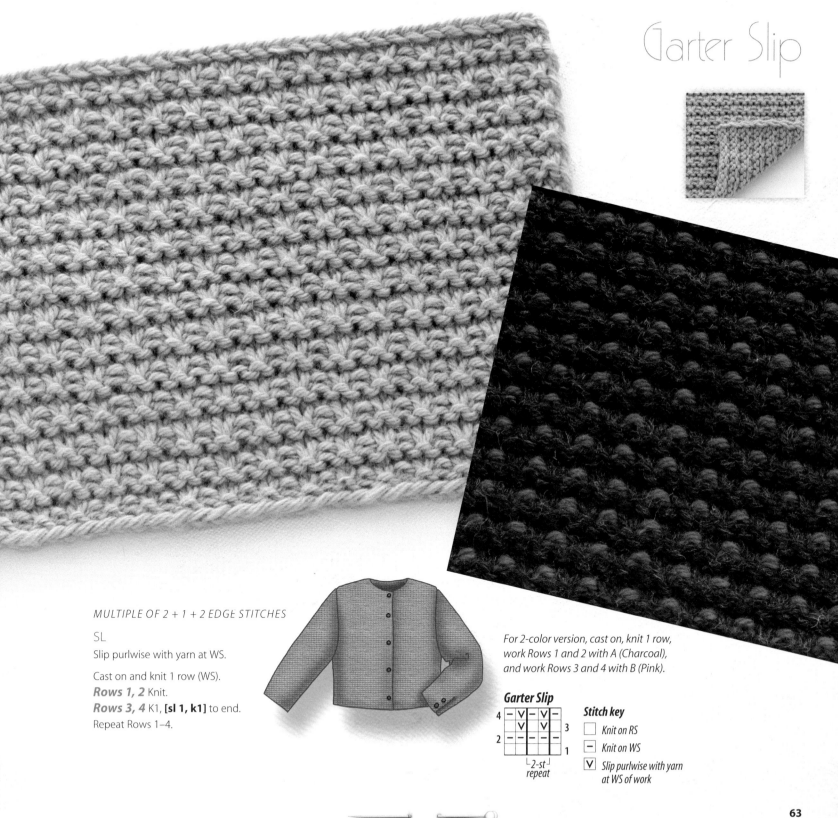

MULTIPLE OF 2 + 1 + 2 EDGE STITCHES

SL
Slip purlwise with yarn at WS.

Cast on and knit 1 row (WS).
Rows 1, 2 Knit.
Rows 3, 4 K1, **[sl 1, k1]** to end.
Repeat Rows 1–4.

For 2-color version, cast on, knit 1 row,
work Rows 1 and 2 with A (Charcoal),
and work Rows 3 and 4 with B (Pink).

Garter Slip

Stitch key

☐ Knit on RS

— Knit on WS

Ⅴ Slip purlwise with yarn at WS of work

2-st repeat

Tri-color Seed

A 2-row stitch pattern and 3-row color sequence (A, B, C) results in a 6-row repeat. Alternating knits and purls blend the colors.

Tri-color Seed

6		5
4		3
2		1

└ 2-st ┘
repeat

MULTIPLE OF 2 + 2 EDGE STITCHES
Worked with 3 colors: A (Purple), B (Blue), and C (Red).

With A, cast on and knit 1 row.
Row 1 (RS) With A, k1, **[k1, p1]** to last stitch, k1.
Row 2 With B, k1, **[p1, k1]** to last stitch, k1.
Row 3 (RS) With C, k1, **[k1, p1]** to last stitch, k1.
Row 4 With A, k1, **[p1, k1]** to last stitch, k1.
Row 5 (RS) With B, k1, **[k1, p1]** to last stitch, k1.
Row 6 With C, k1, **[p1, k1]** to last stitch, k1.
Repeat Rows 1–6.

Stitch key

☐ Knit on RS, purl on WS

⊟ Purl on RS, knit on WS

Color key

☐ A

▨ B

▩ C

stitches for TAILORED knits

Colored Seed

Colored Seed

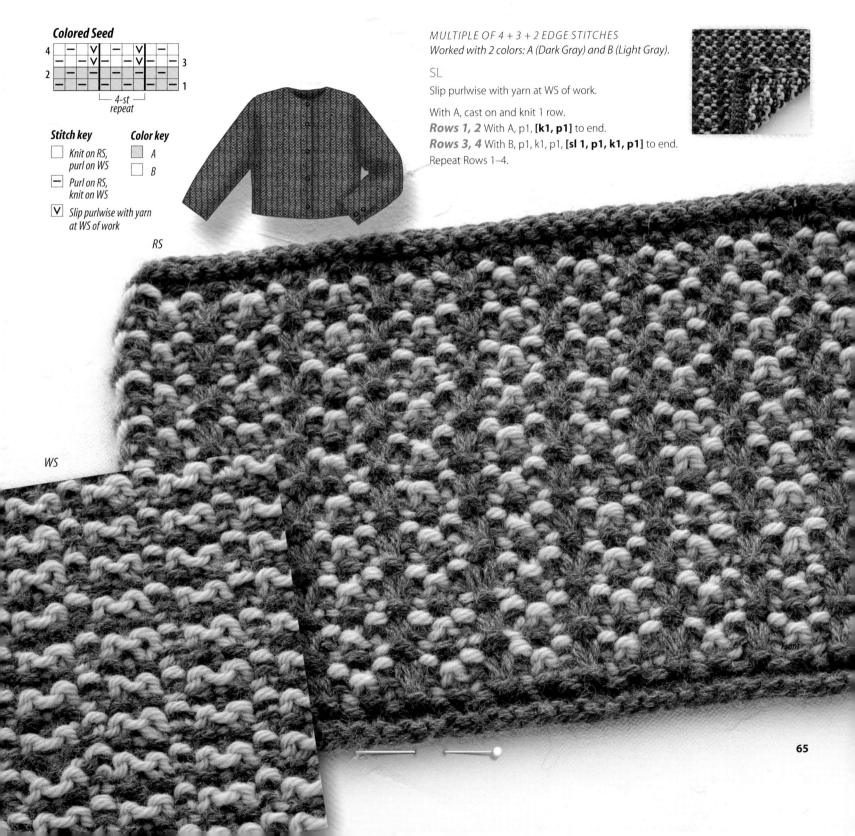

4		−		V		−		−	V			
	−		V	−			−		V	−		3
2		−		V		−		−	V			
	−		−			−		−		−		1

4-st repeat

Stitch key

☐ Knit on RS, purl on WS

− Purl on RS, knit on WS

V Slip purlwise with yarn at WS of work

Color key

☐ A

☐ B

RS

WS

MULTIPLE OF 4 + 3 + 2 EDGE STITCHES
Worked with 2 colors: A (Dark Gray) and B (Light Gray).

SL
Slip purlwise with yarn at WS of work.

With A, cast on and knit 1 row.
Rows 1, 2 With A, p1, **[k1, p1]** to end.
Rows 3, 4 With B, p1, k1, p1, **[sl 1, p1, k1, p1]** to end.
Repeat Rows 1–4.

English Rose

K1B (KNIT IN ROW BELOW)

1 Instead of working into next stitch on left needle, work into stitch directly below it.

2 Pull stitch off left needle and let it drop.

Knitting in the row below and purling on RS rows breaks up the 2-row bands of color.

English Rose

2-st repeat

Stitch key

☐ Knit on RS

− Purl on RS, knit on WS

↓ K1b

Color key

☐ A

▨ B

▨ C

MULTIPLE OF 2 + 2 EDGE STITCHES
Worked with 3 colors: A (Purple), B (Blue), and C (Lavender).

With C, cast on and knit 1 row.
Row 1 (RS) With A, k1, **[p1, k1b]** to last stitch, k1.
Row 2 With A, knit.
Row 3 With B, k1, k1b, **[p1, k1b]** to last 2 stitches, p1, k1.
Row 4 With B, knit.
Rows 5, 6 With C, repeat Rows 1–2.
Rows 7, 8 With A, repeat Rows 3–4.
Rows 9, 10 With B, repeat Rows 1–2.
Rows 11, 12 With C, repeat Rows 3–4.
Repeat Rows 1–12.

stitches for TAILORED knits

Fleck Tweed

Flecked Tweed Stitch

4-st repeat

Stitch key
☐ Knit on RS, purl on WS
– Knit on WS
⊻ Slip purlwise with yarn at RS of work
⩔ Slip purlwise with yarn at WS of work

Color key
☐ A
☐ B

MULTIPLE OF 4 + 3 + 2 EDGE STITCHES
Worked with 2 colors: A (Black) and B (White).

SL
Slip purlwise with yarn to the back of work (at RS on WS rows, at WS on RS rows).

With A, cast on and knit 2 rows.
Row 1 (WS) With A, k1, p1, **[sl 1, p3]** to last 3 stitches, sl 1, p1, k1.
Row 2 With A, k2, **[sl 1, k3]** to last 3 stitches, sl 1, k2.
Row 3 With B, k1, p3, **[sl 1, p3]** to last stitch, k1.
Row 4 With B, k4, **[sl 1, k3]** to last stitch, k1.
Repeat Rows 1–4.

2-color Texture

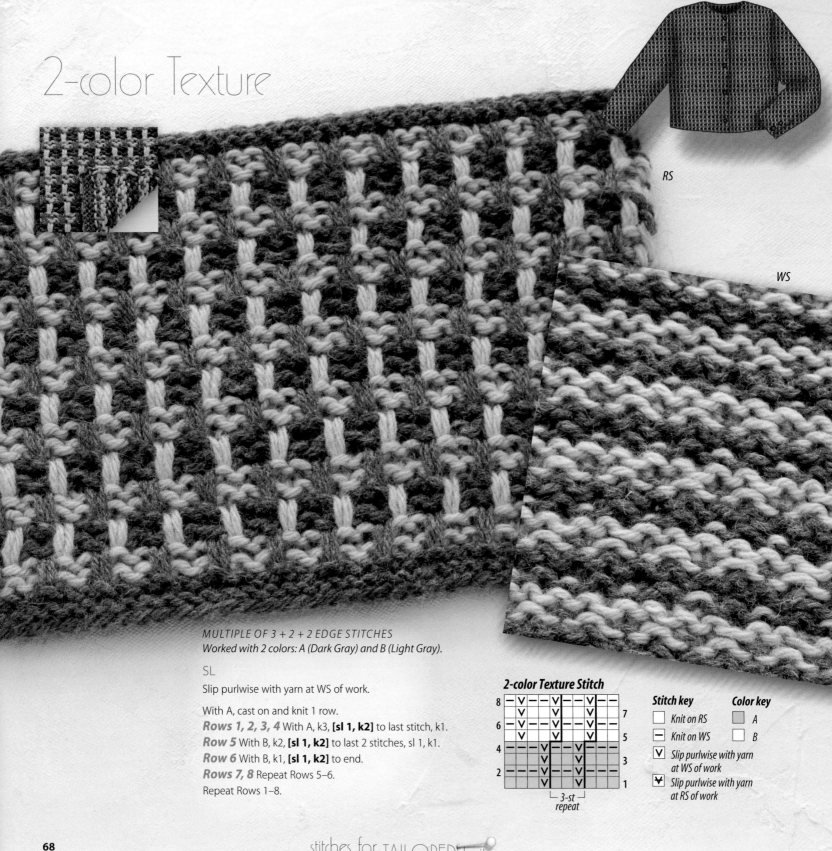

RS

WS

MULTIPLE OF 3 + 2 + 2 EDGE STITCHES
Worked with 2 colors: A (Dark Gray) and B (Light Gray).

SL
Slip purlwise with yarn at WS of work.

With A, cast on and knit 1 row.
Rows 1, 2, 3, 4 With A, k3, **[sl 1, k2]** to last stitch, k1.
Row 5 With B, k2, **[sl 1, k2]** to last 2 stitches, sl 1, k1.
Row 6 With B, k1, **[sl 1, k2]** to end.
Rows 7, 8 Repeat Rows 5–6.
Repeat Rows 1–8.

2-color Texture Stitch

Stitch key

☐	Knit on RS
—	Knit on WS
V	Slip purlwise with yarn at WS of work
⩔	Slip purlwise with yarn at RS of work

Color key

▨	A
☐	B

3-st repeat

Slip-stitch Fabric

```
8  —
6  —        ⋎⋎      ⋎⋎
           ⋎⋎      ⋎⋎            7
4  —                              5
2  —    ⋎⋎      ⋎⋎      ⋎⋎
        ⋎⋎      ⋎⋎      ⋎⋎        3
                                  1
        └ 4-st ┘
          repeat
```

MULTIPLE OF 4 + 2 EDGE STITCHES
Worked with 2 colors: A (Brown) and B (Tan).

SL
Slip purlwise with yarn at RS of work.

With A, cast on and knit 1 row.
Row 1 (RS) With A, k2, **[sl 2, k2]** to end.
Row 2 With A, k1, p1, **[sl 2, p2]** to last 4 stitches, sl 2, p1, k1.
Row 3 With A, knit.
Row 4 With A, k1, purl to last stitch, k1.
Row 5 With B, k4, **[sl 2, k2]** to last 2 stitches, k2.
Row 6 With B, k1, p3, **[sl 2, p2]** to last 2 stitches, p1, k1.
Row 7 With B, knit.
Row 8 With B, k1, purl to last stitch, k1.
Repeat Rows 1–8.

Slip-stitch Check

MULTIPLE OF 3 + 2 + 2 EDGE STITCHES
Worked with 2 colors: A (Black) and B (White).

SL
Slip purlwise with yarn at WS of work.

With A, cast on and knit 1 row.
Row 1 (RS) With A, knit.
Row 2 With A, k1, purl to last stitch, k1.
Row 3 With B, k3, **[sl 1, k2]** to last stitch, k1.
Row 4 With B, k1, p2, **[sl 1, p2]** to last stitch, k1.
Repeat Rows 1–4.

Slip-stitch Check

			V		V		—	
				V		V		
—							—	

└ 3-st ┘
repeat

Stitch key

☐ Knit on RS,
purl on WS

— Knit on WS

V Slip purlwise with yarn
at WS of work

Color key

▨ A

☐ B

stitches for TAILORED knits

Dice Check

Dice Check

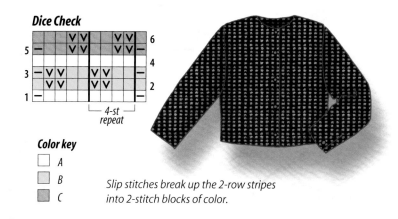

L—— 4-st repeat ——J

Color key
- ☐ A
- ▨ B
- ▨ C

Slip stitches break up the 2-row stripes into 2-stitch blocks of color.

MULTIPLE OF 4 + 2 EDGE STITCHES
Worked with 3 colors: A (Dark Gray),
B (Light Gray), and C (Rust).

SL
Slip purlwise with yarn at WS of work.

With A, cast on and knit 2 rows.
Row 1 (WS) With A, k1, purl to last stitch, k1.
Row 2 With B, k1, **[k2, sl 2]** to last stitch, k1.
Row 3 With B, k1, **[sl 2, p2]** to last stitch, k1.
Row 4 With A, knit.
Row 5 With C, k1, **[p2, sl 2]** to last stitch, k1.
Row 6 With C, k1, **[sl 2, k2]** to last stitch, k1.
Repeat Rows 1–6.

Chatelaine

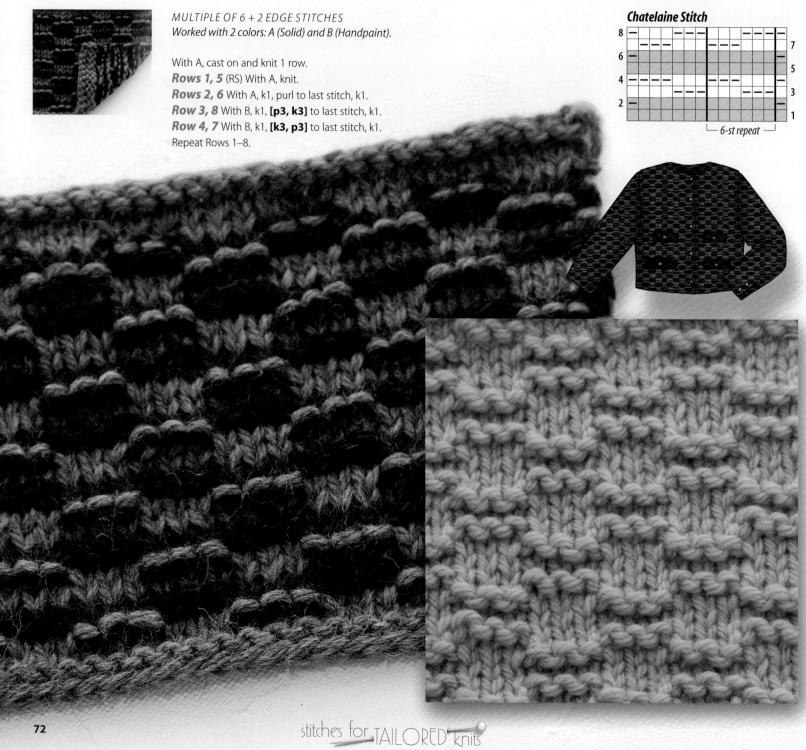

MULTIPLE OF 6 + 2 EDGE STITCHES
Worked with 2 colors: A (Solid) and B (Handpaint).

With A, cast on and knit 1 row.
Rows 1, 5 (RS) With A, knit.
Rows 2, 6 With A, k1, purl to last stitch, k1.
Row 3, 8 With B, k1, **[p3, k3]** to last stitch, k1.
Row 4, 7 With B, k1, **[k3, p3]** to last stitch, k1.
Repeat Rows 1–8.

Chatelaine Stitch

6-st repeat

stitches for TAILORED knits

Purl 2-by-2

Purl 2-by-2

4	—				—				—
			—				—			3
2	—				—				—
			—				—			1

└─ 4-st ─┘
repeat

Stitch key

☐ Knit on RS,
   purl on WS

⊟ Purl on RS,
   knit on WS

Color key

▨ A

☐ B

MULTIPLE OF 4 + 2 (INCLUDES EDGE STITCHES)
Worked with 2 colors, A (Solid) and B (Handpaint).

With A, cast on and knit 1 row.
Alternate 2 rows A and 2 rows B.
All rows K2, **[p2, k2]** to end.

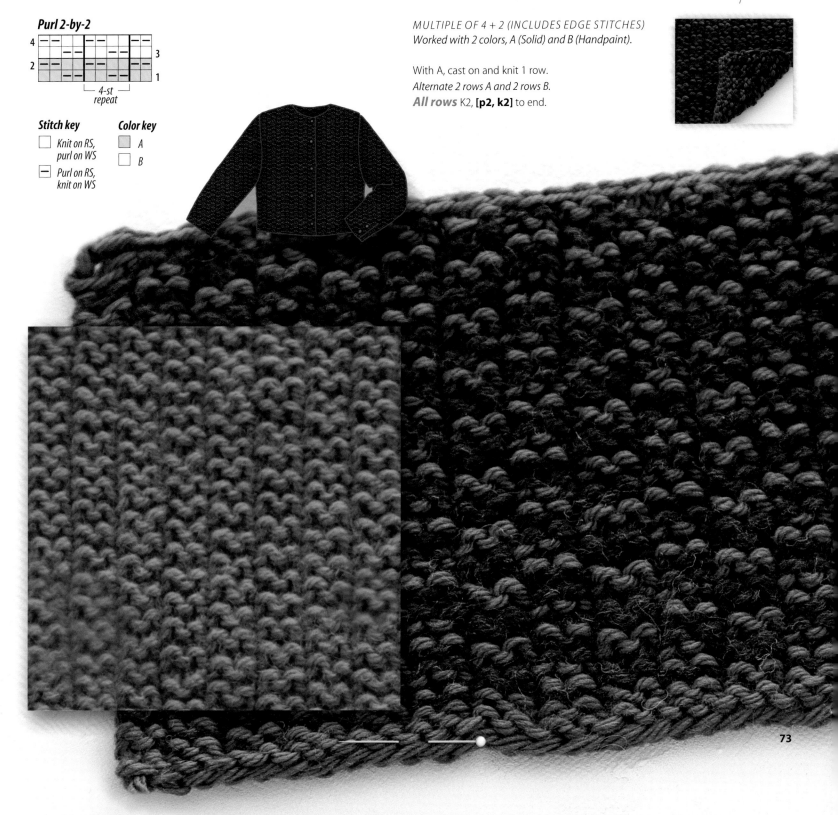

73

Quilted Fabrics

Traditionally, quilting stitches connect 2 or 3 layers of material together to make a thicker fabric. The original purpose was for warmth or protection.

Coco Chanel would stabilize the loosely woven fabrics she used in her jackets and suits by quilting the lining to the outer layer. This quilting eventually became decorative. In 1955, her signature 2.55 quilted bag was released and is still popular today. You will find its diamond pattern repeated in other Chanel products, and it inspires many designer lines.

In knitting, this diagonal grid can be replicated using knits and purls, slipped-stitch floats, and elongated stitches. These patterns are a true homage to the design legend and her iconic style.

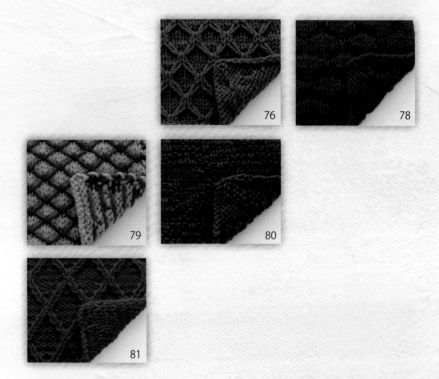

stitches for TAILORED knits

Diamond Brocade

Diamond Brocade

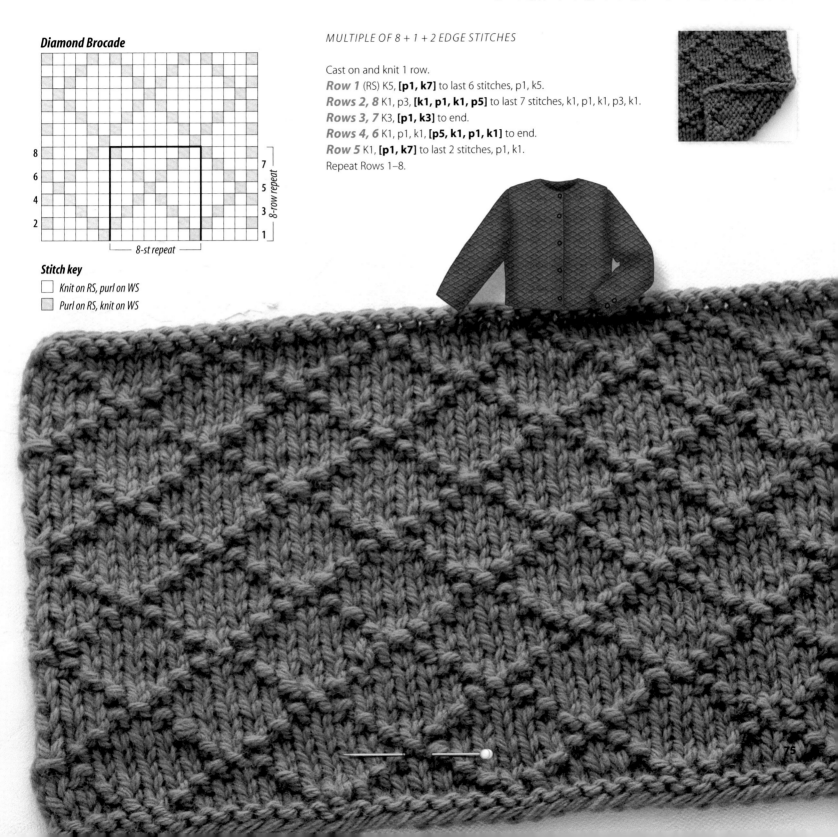

8
6
4
2

7
5
3
1

8-row repeat

8-st repeat

Stitch key

☐ Knit on RS, purl on WS

▨ Purl on RS, knit on WS

MULTIPLE OF 8 + 1 + 2 EDGE STITCHES

Cast on and knit 1 row.
Row 1 (RS) K5, **[p1, k7]** to last 6 stitches, p1, k5.
Rows 2, 8 K1, p3, **[k1, p1, k1, p5]** to last 7 stitches, k1, p1, k1, p3, k1.
Rows 3, 7 K3, **[p1, k3]** to end.
Rows 4, 6 K1, p1, k1, **[p5, k1, p1, k1]** to end.
Row 5 K1, **[p1, k7]** to last 2 stitches, p1, k1.
Repeat Rows 1–8.

English Diamond

MULTIPLE OF 6 + 2 EDGE STITCHES

SL
Slip purlwise with yarn at WS of work.

Cast on and knit 2 rows.
Row 1 (WS) K1, purl to last stitch, k1.
Row 2 K3, **[k2 with double wrap, k4]** to last 5 stitches, k2 with double wrap, k3.
Row 3 K1, p2, **[sl 2 dropping extra wraps, p4]** to last 5 stitches, sl 2 dropping extra wraps, p2, k1.
Row 4 K3, **[sl 2, k4]** to last 5 stitches, sl 2, k3.
Row 5 K1, p2, **[sl 2, p4]** to last 5 stitches, sl 2, p2, k1.
Row 6 K1, **[1/2 Elongated RC, 1/2 Elongated LC]** to last stitch, k1.
Row 7 K1, purl to last stitch, k1.

Row 8 K1, k1 with double wrap, k4, **[k2 with double wrap, k4]** to last 2 stitches, k1 with double wrap, k1.
Row 9 K1, sl 1 dropping extra wrap, p4, **[sl 2 dropping extra wraps, p4]** to last 2 stitches, sl 1 dropping extra wrap, k1.
Row 10 K1, sl 1, k4, **[sl 2, k4]** to last 2 stitches, sl 1, k1.
Row 11 K1, sl 1, p4, **[sl 2, p4]** to last 2 stitches, sl 1, k1.
Row 12 K1, **[1/2 Elongated LC, 1/2 Elongated RC]** to last stitch, k1.
Repeat Rows 1–12.

English Diamond

6-st repeat

Stitch key

☐ Knit on RS, purl on WS

— Knit on WS

Ⅴ Slip purlwise with yarn at WS of work

Ⅴ Slip purlwise with yarn at WS of work, dropping extra wrap

⅋ Knit with double wrap

⟋⟍ **1/2 Elongated RC**

⟍⟋ **1/2 Elongated LC**

DOUBLE WRAP

1 Knit 1, EXCEPT wrap yarn twice around needle before drawing new stitch through old stitch.

ELONGATED STITCH

2 On next row, slip the stitch, dropping extra wrap as stitch is pulled off left needle.

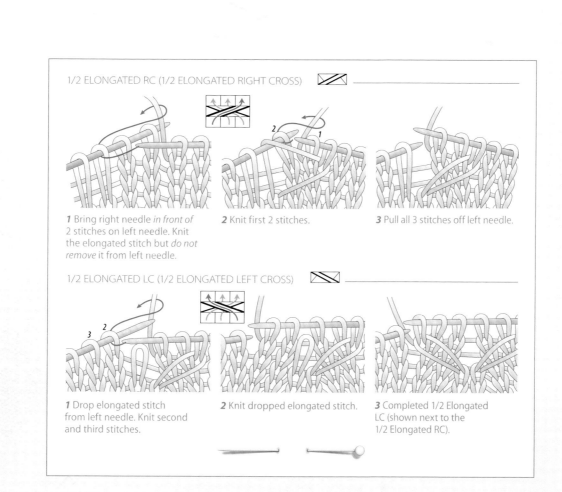

1/2 ELONGATED RC (1/2 ELONGATED RIGHT CROSS)

1 Bring right needle *in front of* 2 stitches on left needle. Knit the elongated stitch but *do not remove* it from left needle.

2 Knit first 2 stitches.

3 Pull all 3 stitches off left needle.

1/2 ELONGATED LC (1/2 ELONGATED LEFT CROSS)

1 Drop elongated stitch from left needle. Knit second and third stitches.

2 Knit dropped elongated stitch.

3 Completed 1/2 Elongated LC (shown next to the 1/2 Elongated RC).

Dip Stitch

MULTIPLE OF 6 + 5 + 2 EDGE STITCHES

Cast on and knit 1 row. Work 6 rows stockinette.

Row 1 (RS) K3, DS, **[k5, DS]** to last 3 stitches, k3.

Row 2 and all WS rows K1, purl to last stitch, k1.

Rows 3, 5, 9, 11 Knit.

Row 7 K6, **[DS, k5]** to last stitch, k1.

Repeat Rows 1–12.

Dip Stitch

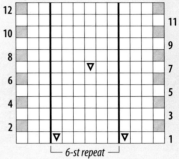

6-st repeat

Stitch key

☐ Knit on RS, purl on WS

▨ Knit on WS

▽ Dip stitch

DS (DIP STITCH)

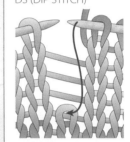

Remove next stitch from left needle and unravel 4 rows.

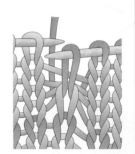

Knit this stitch, catching the ladders.

RS

WS

Royal Quilting

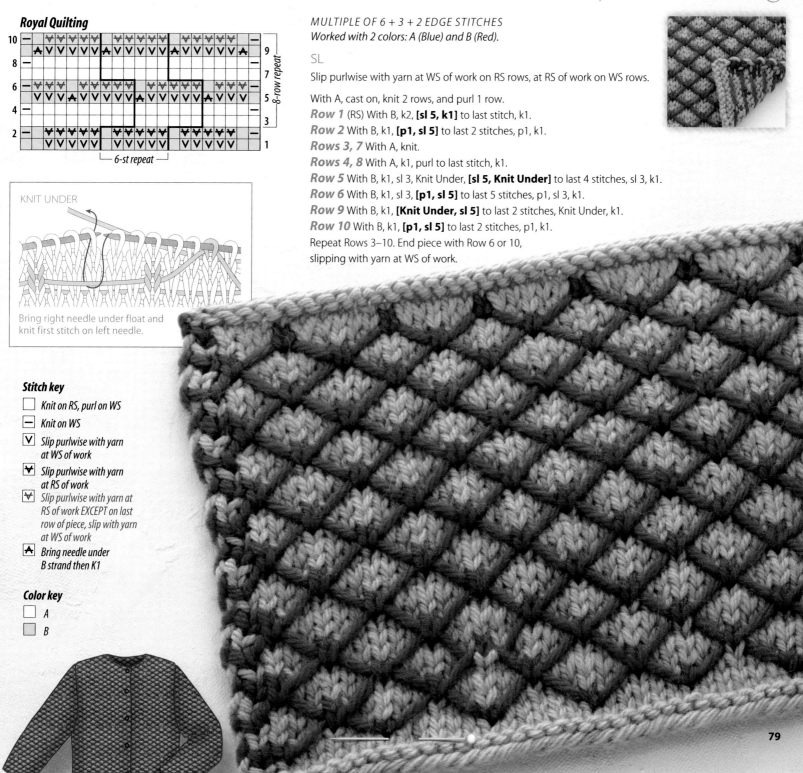

Stitch key

- ☐ Knit on RS, purl on WS
- — Knit on WS
- V Slip purlwise with yarn at WS of work
- ☒ Slip purlwise with yarn at RS of work
- ☒ Slip purlwise with yarn at RS of work EXCEPT on last row of piece, slip with yarn at WS of work
- ⚹ Bring needle under B strand then K1

Color key

- ☐ A
- ☐ B

KNIT UNDER

Bring right needle under float and knit first stitch on left needle.

MULTIPLE OF 6 + 3 + 2 EDGE STITCHES
Worked with 2 colors: A (Blue) and B (Red).

SL
Slip purlwise with yarn at WS of work on RS rows, at RS of work on WS rows.

With A, cast on, knit 2 rows, and purl 1 row.
Row 1 (RS) With B, k2, **[sl 5, k1]** to last stitch, k1.
Row 2 With B, k1, **[p1, sl 5]** to last 2 stitches, p1, k1.
Rows 3, 7 With A, knit.
Rows 4, 8 With A, k1, purl to last stitch, k1.
Row 5 With B, k1, sl 3, Knit Under, **[sl 5, Knit Under]** to last 4 stitches, sl 3, k1.
Row 6 With B, k1, sl 3, **[p1, sl 5]** to last 5 stitches, p1, sl 3, k1.
Row 9 With B, k1, **[Knit Under, sl 5]** to last 2 stitches, Knit Under, k1.
Row 10 With B, k1, **[p1, sl 5]** to last 2 stitches, p1, k1.
Repeat Rows 3–10. End piece with Row 6 or 10,
slipping with yarn at WS of work.

79

Diamond Moss

MULTIPLE OF 10 + 1 + 2 EDGE STITCHES

Cast on and knit 1 row.

Row 1 (RS) K1, p2, **[k7, p3]** to last 10 stitches, k7, p2, k1.

Row 2 and all WS Rows K1, purl to last stitch, k1.

Rows 3, 19 K1, p3, k5, **[p5, k5]** to last 4 stitches, p3, k1.

Rows 5, 17 K2, **[p3, k3, p3, k1]** to last stitch, k1.

Rows 7, 15 **[K3, p3, k1, p3]** to last 3 stitches, k3.

Rows 9, 13 K4, **[p5, k5]** to last 9 stitches, p5, k4.

Row 11 K5, **[p3, k7]** to last 8 stitches, p3, k5.

Repeat Rows 1–20.

Diamond Moss

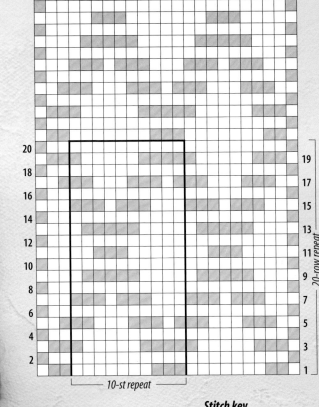

Stitch key

☐	Knit on RS, purl on WS
▨	Purl on RS, knit on WS
⧄	1/1 RC
⧄	1/1 RPC
⧅	1/1 LPC

Diamond Lattice

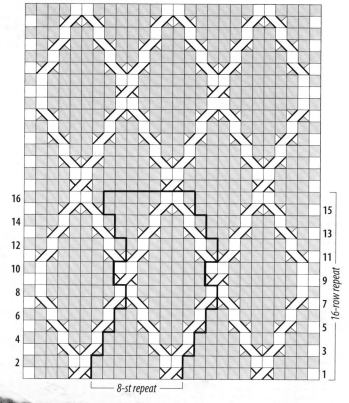

16
14
12
10
8
6
4
2

15
13
11
9
7
5
3
1

16-row repeat

8-st repeat

MULTIPLE OF 8 + 2 EDGE STITCHES

1/1 LPC
Slip 1 to cable needle, hold to front, p1; k1 from cable needle.

1/1 RC
Work as for 1/1 RPC EXCEPT knit first stitch. See illustration page 28.

Cast on and knit 1 row.
Row 1 (RS) K1, p3, **[1/1 RC, p6]** to last 6 stitches, 1/1 RC, p3, k1.
Row 2 and all WS rows K1, knit the knits and purl the purls to last stitch, k1.
Row 3 K1, p2, **[1/1 RPC, 1/1 LPC, p4]** to last 7 stitches, 1/1 RPC, 1/1 LPC, p2, k1.
Row 5 K1, p1, **[1/1 RPC, p2, 1/1 LPC, p2]** to last 8 stitches, 1/1 RPC, p2, 1/1 LPC, p1, k1.
Row 7 K1, **[1/1 RPC, p4, 1/1 LPC]** to last stitch, k1.
Row 9 K2, **[p6, 1/1 RC]** to last 8 stitches, p6, k2.
Row 11 K1, **[1/1 LPC, p4, 1/1 RPC]** to last stitch, k1.
Row 13 K1, p1, **[1/1 LPC, p2, 1/1 RPC, p2]** to last 8 stitches, 1/1 LPC, p2, 1/1 RPC, p1, k1.
Row 15 K1, p2, **[1/1 LPC, 1/1 RPC, p4]** to last 7 stitches, 1/1 LPC, 1/1 RPC, p2, k1.
Repeat Rows 1–16.

1/1 RPC (1/1 RIGHT PURL CROSS)

1 Bring right needle *in front of* first stitch on left needle. Knit second stitch but *do not remove* it from left needle.

2 Purl first stitch.

3 Pull both stitches off left needle.

Techniques

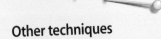

Other techniques

1/1 LC	28
1/1 LPC	81
1/1 RC	28
1/1 RC (WS row)	60
1/1 RPC	81
1/1 RSC	51
1/2 LC	40
1/2 RC	40
2/2 LC	35
2/2 RC	35
Cluster stitch	54
Dip stitch	78
Double wrap	77
Elongated stitch	77
Fancy slip	50
Knit in row below (k1b)	66
Knit through back loop (k1 tbl)	45
Knit under	55
Sl 1. k1, yo, psso	61

YO (YARN OVER)

Bring yarn under needle to the front, take it over the needle to the back, and knit the next stitch.

Completed yo increase.

SSK

1 Slip 2 stitches **separately** to right needle as if to knit.

2 Slip left needle into these 2 stitches from left to right and knit them together: 2 stitches become 1.

The result is a left-slanting decrease.

P3TOG

1 Insert right needle into first 3 stitches on left needle.
2 Purl all 3 stitches together, as if they were 1. The result is a right-slanting double decrease.

Repeats by the number

2-stitch

English Rose	66
English Tweed	61
Garter Slip	63
Half Linen Stitch	37
Pebbles	55
Speckle Rib	58
Tiny Houndstooth	44, 45
Tri-color Seed	64

3-stitch

2-color Texture	68
Cluster Stitch	54
Diagonal Lace	24
Fancy Slip Houndstooth	50
Slip-stitch Check	70
Small Houndstooth	43
Twisted Texture	60

4-stitch

2-by-2 Diagonal Rib	25
2-color Diagonal	30
Big Houndstooth	46, 47
Brick Stitch	57
Broken Rib	53
Cabled Basketweave	35
Colored Seed	65
Diagonal Basket	40
Diagonal Rib	23
Dice Check	71
Fleck Tweed	67
Houndstooth Check	51

Slip-stitch Basketweave	36
Slip-stitch Fabric	69
Purl 2-by-2	73
Trinity Stitch	56
Woven Basketweave	34

6-stitch

Chatelaine	72
Dip Stitch	78
English Diamond	76
Relief Diagonal	28
Royal Quilting	79
Stranded Basketweave	38
Woven Diagonal	27

7-stitch

Diamond Houndstooth	48

8-stitch

Diamond Brocade	75
Diamond Lattice	81
Giant Houndstooth	49
Irish Basketweave	33
K4-P4 Diagonal	26
Ladder Basketweave	39

10-stitch

Arrowhead	31
Diamond Moss	80
Mosaic Basketweave	41

SKP (sl 1-k1-psso)

 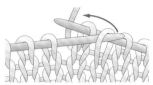 

1 Slip 1 stitch knitwise from left needle onto right needle.
2 Knit 1 as usual.

3 Pass slipped stitch over knit stitch: 2 stitches become 1.

The result is a left-slanting decrease.

SLIP PURLWISE

1 Insert right needle into next stitch on left needle from back to front (as if to purl).

2 Slide stitch from left to right needle. *Stitch orientation* does not change (right leg of stitch loop is at front of needle).

The stitch slipped purlwise can be a knit or a purl.

SLIP KNITWISE

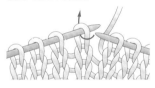  

1 Insert right needle into next stitch on left needle from front to back (as if to knit).

2 Slide stitch from left to right needle. *Stitch orientation* changes (right leg of stitch loop is at back of needle).

The stitch slipped knitwise can be a knit or a purl.

SLIP WITH YARN ON RIGHT SIDE OF WORK

Move the yarn to the *front* on a right-side row…

… or to the *back* on a wrong-side row before slipping a stitch. This places the yarn on the right side of the fabric.

stitches for TAILORED knits

stitches for TAILORED knits